Run Your Own Race

Run Your Own Race

Happiness after 50

BARB ROCK

TATE PUBLISHING
AND ENTERPRISES, LLC

Published by Tate Publishing & Enterprises, LLC
127 E. Trade Center Terrace | Mustang, Oklahoma 73064 USA
1.888.361.9473 | www.tatepublishing.com

Tate Publishing is committed to excellence in the publishing industry. The company reflects the philosophy established by the founders, based on Psalm 68:11,
"The Lord gave the word and great was the company of those who published it."

Book design copyright © 2015 by Tate Publishing, LLC. All rights reserved.
Cover design by Eileen Cueno
Interior design by Jake Muelle

Published in the United States of America

ISBN: 978-1-63268-131-7
Family & Relationships / General
14.11.19

Barb Rock has had many careers! Early in her twenties she began teaching aerobic dance, which lasted about ten years, later opening a nail salon in Lakewood for nine years, and then had an extensive career in real estate until her retirement in 2011. Barb is currently playing drums with two professional bands. One is a Motown band and the other a classic rock band. But Barb's biggest passion and accomplishment was utilizing her degree in counseling. Barb has been helping others to see a new perspective, whether they are young teenagers, married couple, or an individual struggling with grief or depression. By providing counseling services at the Oasis of Hope Center in Tacoma, she has seen the growth and changes in her clients' lives just by using a positive approach. By applying basic psychology and adapting to our human tendencies, Barb used her insight and experiences to write this book for women who are fifty or older and approaching retirement. She has talked firsthand to hundreds of women who have battled weight issues while attending her aerobic classes. While doing nails, her clients have shared tears and details about personal trauma and finally the big money issues she helped thousands of home buyers and homeowners face during her successful real estate career. She considers herself retired even while playing in two bands, having a small counseling practice, and writing this book. Barb has seen the pain, the hurt, and humiliation from exhausted, lonely women. Retirement is a new beginning for life with new routines. Embracing retirement and menopause, Barb deeply believes, will provide understanding so women can give themselves permission to enjoy life and be happy, respecting who they are and who they have become. It is finally time to run your own race!

Letter from Copy Editor at Tate Publishing

This is a very honest and useful book about life in your fifties, the many issues that you face, and the necessary skills and knowledge to cope effectively. I believe that many women will find this valuable as they try to understand and cope. It will also be very useful to men who want to understand women. The information included sound well researched and backed by reputable sources. I do admire the way you've used your personal issues like your separation with your spouse and probable divorce in a positive endeavor that can help millions of women out there who may be going through the same problems. The courage and logic that led into writing this book and sharing it with others portray the winning attitude that you possess, and I know that whatever your decision will be, God will be on your side.

- The book is very entertaining (i.e., with the stories and analogies) and full of valuable information.
- It is quite well written and well organized.
- It is valuable to both men and women, young and old.

That being said, you have proven your mastery at writing, and I commend you. Thank you for allowing us to work with you and your story. We are truly honored, and I personally enjoyed your story.

Warmest regards,
Flordeline

Contents

Preface

Achieving Happiness
at Fifty Plus

This book is designed to help women, like myself, clearly identify their strengths and weaknesses and take time to embrace a new perspective for their lives at age fifty. Moving through retirement, menopause, and empty-nest issues as well as other changes such as divorce can be difficult and overwhelming. We face challenges we have never encountered before, but regardless of our temperament or personality, we can adapt and face these challenges by running our own race. We must all run our lives the way we choose. Our lives are a big race!

Hopefully there will be some insights on many of these subjects, and new thoughts and ideas may come about, helping us see who we really are and how we can be happy exactly where we are.

Having a master's degree on philosophy in counseling allows me to understand how we may think a certain way and why we may think a certain way, but my goal is utilizing our options and using our imagination to create a better and happier outcome, resulting in a happier life as we go through the change of life. While counseling women and couples, I can see some of the efforts women make. Unfortunately it is often accomplished with misguided direction. How we approach things in our life and our interaction through our daily lives can be completely dependent on how we think about things. A different viewpoint can help us create new habits and a new mind-set to allow us to be happy no matter what we are facing.

We can all be average or basically happy, but to be above average and very happy is much harder. But using practical strategies and techniques it can be very easy. Run your own race means just that…run your own race. There is an old saying: you live in your thirties and forties worrying on what people are thinking about you, and when you get into your fifties and sixties, you find out nobody was thinking about you. They were too busy thinking about themselves. We each run our own lives differently, and life is a big race. One big, long race! Just like a road racetrack, the track goes in many different directions. I will use a lot of car analogies in my book because I identify with how a car is a fine and intricate machine that needs maintenance and care. But a car can easily become out of tune. With wear and tear and some big bumps to go over or around, a car must be tuned continuously. We, as individuals, also must be tuned, especially in this changing atmosphere of living and technology we are continually adapting to.

By age fifty we are smarter—well, most of us—but we have learned from the school of hard knocks. If you are driving on the freeway going north and you wanted to go south, what would you do? You would immediately turn around. Driving through life is no different. Sometimes ideas come from a different perspective. A situation or frustration may have a creative solution that you may not have thought about. It is said necessity is the creator of motivation and invention. Without frustration or lack of something, there is no need to make a change or adapt. It is necessary for your happiness as you go into menopause and retirement to be aware of pitfalls and obstacles you will face.

This book may spark a fire inside you to research something that turns into a solution. This book may allow you to accept a change of attitude or correct a destructive thought pattern, but hopefully it will give you ammunition to believe that life after fifty can be the best time of your life. You may even come up with a great new hobby as a result of reading this book.

Our time here on this earth is so short. What a shame it would be to allow something that happened in our past to ruin one more day.

We naturally tend to view ourselves by what *others* think of us. Our self-esteem is directly linked to how the most important people in our lives view us.

My background and upbringing may be very different or very similar to yours, but the ultimate desire is to shed light on our needs, our outlook on life, past and present, then make some sense of it, making adjustments and strategizing moving forward into our sixties and beyond.

As an extremely motivated, obsessive personality myself, it has worked in my favor at times, and at times to my detriment. But controlling our emotions and learning to pay attention to ourselves, we can learn about ourselves and make good life decisions and create a life to enjoy, instead of just existing.

My goal is to encourage women who are dealing with a new change during their change. Some may be premenopausal, and this will let you have insight to predict what can make it easier when your emotions are out of control due to hormones and circumstances. Things could be modified now for a happier life if you know what to watch for or are warned ahead of time. The *change of life* is simply just that. You already have experienced symptoms such as hot flashes, night sweats, emotional outbreaks, and roller-coaster emotions about trivial things. Most of this is due to hormonal changes. Our frame of mind and how we perceive our lives can predict our future outcome and happiness during these changes. New habits may need to be established to make these changes easier and have happier lives along the way. As the saying goes, life is too short. This book may have some ideas for new habits, patterns of thinking, and just general, honest evaluation of how you can control more of your life than you may be presently doing or even aware of your ability to do so!

Happiness after age fifty should be easy, but it sometimes is packed with so much emotional baggage—years of tolerance, and many years of hurt, indifference, and struggle. Finding happiness can be easy with the right perspective, and I hope that this book will open up our thinking and help us reflect and change as we are going through this change so we can run our own race without comparing ourselves to others or being influenced by others. No one can know who we really are better than ourselves. It takes time and reflection to find out what makes us tick, what makes us cry, and finally what makes us happy.

Introduction

By age fifty and up, most of us have raised our children, been married at least once, and now are looking back on our lives. We all have regrets and memories we would like to remember or just forget. We have spent most of our lives working to take care of our kids, spouses, bosses, and friends. If you have a tendency to always want to please others unselfishly, this becomes your personality. It is so easy to continue the same patterns because as we age we are reluctant to change. We have the mind-set that if it's not broken, don't fix it. It's worked in the past, so why change it now. But by age fifty plus, we really must embrace the notion of doing for ourselves, without regard to what others may think or feel is right for us. We must be willing to look deeply at ourselves and make changes to adapt to our new life at fifty plus. And most of all, we must acknowledge and believe that we are worthy of happiness and not allow anyone to steal our joy for our remaining years! No one!

After I retired from a very hectic real estate career, I had to come to terms with this very thought process. I had been serving people and sacrificing my time and energy solely to my clients, which many times meant skipping meals, sacrificing weekends, even a vague memory of selling a home on Easter morning. I would be coming home at 8:30 or 9:00 p.m. every night, allowing no time for myself, only to get up and start all over again.

Balance

Balance is something that is difficult to attain, especially when you are absorbed in the moment. People who are naturally driven or highly motivated by nature are too focused and have a difficult time finding balance. We all joke and laugh about obsessive-compulsive disorder, but many of us are workaholics, overly conscientious and obsessed with details, mercilessly demanding of ourselves, and feeling guilty with the slightest imperfection. These are common symptoms of OCD. We probably all have a little ADD and OCD at some level, if we are completely honest about it. When we become inflexible and push our expectations onto others, expecting them to be just as conscientious, then it becomes a problem and will cause rifts in many of our relationships. So how can we balance those tendencies without feeling guilty or giving up our sense of happiness? Hopefully I can bring some ideas and new thought patterns that will allow you to be who you are by aiming to understand how biological, behavioral, psychological, and social factors can influence our health and wellness. People are living longer and healthier than ever before. Today, the most common causes of death are strongly related to preventable factors and unhealthy behaviors such as smoking cigarettes, poor diet, sedentary lifestyle, and poor stress-coping skills.

Fortunately we can learn scientifically proven lifestyle skills to make positive, healthy changes in our lives.

I took up playing the drums at age fifty. Every day regardless of my schedule, it was my new balance, something for me. This was great while still working in real estate because it was a good distraction where I could bang on my drums for hours away from all the hassles of escrow problems, lending requirements, and general real estate roadblocks I encountered on a daily, hourly basis. What I would think was twenty minutes was actually over two hours of drum practice. That was a sign! I enjoy it so much that time flew by. Time would pass quickly as I practiced my drums in my room (my poor neighbors!).

Everybody needs something of their own that they enjoy doing therefore balancing their lives by doing it. It can be a hobby, or just reading, but it is fulfilling enough that time flies by very quickly. I needed something to do that would be fulfilling to me that I enjoyed. Something that was so enjoyable that two hours seemed like just twenty minutes. Playing my drums was my *something*. I began lessons and have been playing drums professionally for five years now in two separate bands.

Maybe you can think of something you really enjoy or would enjoy doing on a regular basis that perhaps in the past you haven't had time to do. It's time to begin doing something enjoyable for yourself on a regular basis. Balance your life with something enjoyable that you had to put on hold due to kids, money, or time.

When you retire, you can revisit and reinvent yourself doing something fun to balance your life.

Throttle Back

Part of balance may include making an effort to relax and throttle back. Think of a car gas pedal and you are pushing down on the gas pedal full throttle. You were not letting up for anything. You keep pressing harder and harder continuously on the gas pedal. This feels normal. You have done it for years! That gas pedal has been you, pushing your life through raising your kids and your different jobs and your aging parents whom you may be attending to plus keeping up with all the technology changes and all the obstacles that life presents on your racetrack of life. Here is the secret. Now it is time to let up on the gas pedal. "Throttle back," as my good friend Marty (Alaska Airlines mechanic) would say in airplane language. It's easy. Just pull your foot off the gas pedal and relax back. It is easier said than done. I was raised with lists of chores to do by my mother and grandmother. I was conditioned that fun is accomplishing projects and more gratification comes when accomplishing a task or cleaning project, organizing project or some other work-related task. "Throttle back" doesn't mean "stop everything." Just give yourself time for some balance where the pendulum now swings your way. The balance you may be lacking is doing something you enjoy! Not something expected of you, as in a job or a spouse's expectation. I now believe that doing something you enjoy for yourself is one of the first things that will create balance in a woman fifty plus because so much of our lives have been spent taking care of others.

For me taking up playing the drums worked well because it was somewhat physical and probably the least restricted instrument as far as creative movements and no hard and fast rules. I had always loved Karen Carpenter playing drums while singing and a huge fan of Don Henley as well. My husband of almost thirty years at that time surprised me with a drum kit for Valentines Day in 2008. Being a driven, motivated person by nature, I embraced this gift and passion. It resulted in immediately signing up for lessons and joining a classic rock band by age fifty-one after just a year of private lessons. The following year we had created a second band called Hot Flash, named one night after I had experienced a hot flash during a break when we were performing at a club. I had to excuse myself and walk outside to cool off. Upon returning inside, the guys in the band voted on Hot Flash as the new name for the new band. I gave up lots of TV time in the evenings to achieve the goal of being able to be stage worthy. Many weekends were spent practicing on my drums instead of going out with friends, or leisure activities. I found myself rushing to complete household chores so I could have more practice time. I enjoyed it that much and felt freedom for the first time in years.

There was a struggle, however, with balance. I was so driven to succeed at this newfound hobby and to be finally giving myself permission to do something for me and only me. This seemed selfish, but remember, so much of our lives are spent taking care of others. Not that we begrudge any of it, but our job of raising our children is completed by fifty years old (usually), and our spouses or significant others are mature now and are very capable of running a household or a vacuum cleaner. You have been balancing your family and schedule since you were most likely in your twenties. Now is your time to just balance yourself and enjoy some life. Otherwise, when is it time?

Finding something you enjoy creates the balance pendulum to swing toward happiness. Your happiness is as important as everybody else's happiness. This was very uncomfortable for me to accept at first. Let me repeat. This was very uncomfortable. How could I do this and selfishly take time out for my drum practice instead of making dinner at exactly 5:00 p.m. as I had always done in the past? How could I abandon my husband in the evening and practice for hours instead of relaxing, watching TV with him? I had to endure this guilt silently and this awful sense of shirking of my expected responsibility to be there for my husband, yet choosing to join two professional bands. No more guilt because it made me happy!

Balance is truly the key to every aspect of our lives. No matter if it is weight loss issues, spending issues, health issues, organization issues, addiction issue, or any other area of our lives that we will address in the following chapters individually. This is the reason why balance is my first idea to explore. So let's explore this balance. Find an interest or passion that you really enjoy.

If doing this interest feels like twenty minutes yet it has been two hours, you found it. The balance/happiness pendulum needs to swing your way, even if you work full-time, part-time, are retired or about to retire.

When I was in real estate back in 2001, I would be working on ten to fifteen transactions all at the same time. Calling escrow offices and lenders about each one, taking appointments for new homes to market, showing one or more of my listings daily, and I was going at top speed and what felt like a few hours was actually nine or ten hours. It was a passion. I was enjoying every aspect of it. Yes, it was hard—yes, it was work—but I loved it. I was helping people find and purchase the American dream and making their life better for many years to come. I was creating TV commercials for running ads on television where they actually came out with a camera and makeup crew to shoot the commercial. It was an amazing experience.

I created billboards and had my photo on six billboards rotating all over the Pierce County area. I paid for radio ads on KZOK radio for four years at a cost of $2,000 a month! I was 100 percent invested. It was my passion. My budget for additional advertising was well over $20,000 a year. Interestingly enough, I must say, those billboards and radio and marketing ads stick with people even years after you retire. I discovered this when I had a gentleman at a club my band was playing at recently tell me, "I saw your car outside, and I remember your real estate advertisements on movie screens at a local theater." I had completely forgotten about advertising at a local theater! The theater would have my billboard photo on the screen, holding the photo for exactly fifteen seconds before the movie would begin. Each separate theater room would display my advertisement rotating and cycling through several times before the movie. It featured me standing next to a Windermere Real Estate sign with a house in the background and my bright yellow convertible Chevy SSR car beside me, holding a SOLD sign.

I laughed when this gentleman reminded me of this. I remember how I would even go to the movie theater to see the advertisement just to make sure my advertisement was on the screen for exactly fifteen seconds as agreed upon in the contract and I was getting my money's worth. I still love my yellow SSR convertible car (that was featured in my advertisement)

as it was parked outside hooked to my white band trailer carrying my drums and sound system.

It was a passion to come up with creative ideas to promote my business. Some of it came naturally as I tend to think outside the box, but it made me happy. It made me want to get up in the morning.

If you have been fortunate enough to have done any job with the added pleasure of enjoying the job, you know about passion and the sense of satisfaction that results from hard work and accomplishment. But when it consumes you and becomes very unbalanced, the happiness pendulum is swinging away from you instead of toward you.

When we are finally fifty plus and retiring from our job or careers or considering retiring, we need to take care to ponder what makes us happy and what makes us want to get up in the morning. Even a stay-at-home parent needs to have something that gives her a passion and sense of accomplishment. Just existing can result in resentment, anger, and even depression. Depression unrecognized or ignored will eat us up, make us fat, and shorten our lives, not to mention make us unhappy.

Personally when I retired, it felt like I was retiring from racing a car driving at two hundred miles per hour at Daytona with my concentration level at full power to sitting in a children's seat at a fair ride going in a slow circle at a slow crawl. My drums were my life-saving balancing tool. It saved me from the whiplash I would have experienced on instantly letting go to retire.

Find your passion. Google subjects you are interested in. We live in a technical world with so much opportunity

BARB ROCK

to get information and ideas to pursue our dreams or utilize our skills or interests. Why not take advantage of this technology and the Internet? We can now speak into our phones and have the Internet connect us to any website. Speak into our phones making a grocery list and voice activate a text to someone. Hurray for technology to make our lives easier, and better, so let's embrace it, not fight it. Recipes at the touch of a screen is amazing since our mothers had to get out the Betty Crocker cookbook to find a recipe.

Make a list of everything you love. I love NASCAR racing. My younger sister and I have followed NASCAR together for years, in our twenties and thirties, and still do to this day. We were loyal Dale Earnhardt fans, and we both shed some tears when he died instantly at Daytona Super Speedway. Our fun weekends would consist of my young son and nephew watching NASCAR all day Saturday, which would include a big plate of nachos and Diet Coke! It was a fun time with my sister, and it lasted all day. So NASCAR would be on my list of what I love and enjoy.

What would your list of things you love consist of? Stop right now and write down a list of things you enjoy or absolutely love.

Attitude

Attitude is such a difficult thing at age fifty plus. Have you noticed how you are less tolerant? Stupid people irritate you? Common sense is not so common! You've seen so much in your life, and you have discovered what

28

you like and don't like on so many levels. What food you like, what activities you enjoy, and the list goes on. Our attitude or approach on life can be so conditioned by habits of thinking. That is the reason change is very difficult as we get older.

What You Think…You Become!

This has to be my ultimate favorite saying. I keep this quote in a picture frame in my drum room. Our minds are much more powerful than we realize. My subconscious reads it even if I don't consciously read it. Did you know, for example, if you simply hold a pencil in your mouth sideways, bringing your lips up and around the pencil making you smile, it actually releases dopamine in your brain, causing your brain to register a smile and makes you feel happy? When you smile at another person first and they smile back, your brain registers a mirror effect to that other person when you smiled, and they *have* to smile back at you. If you try this experiment at the grocery store or out in public, you will see this happen. So if you think you are a happy person, you will become a happy person. Here are a few suggestions I read from an author who wrote a book on happiness.

For twenty-one days straight (It takes twenty-one days to create a habit):

- Buy a journal.
  Write three things you are grateful for every day. It can be anything in your life you are grateful for. An example: Traffic went my

way, a check came in the mail just in time, or a problem turned out better than expected. Even what seems insignificant can be acknowledged if you are looking for it.

- Add three smiles to your day every day for twenty-one days. When you are at the bank passing by someone, smile at them, in the checkout line or simply taking a walk. Your brain smiles before you actually smile.

- Take fifteen minutes every day to do something to have fun. Something you enjoy and decide to do it just fifteen minutes every day.

- Recharge your battery with meaningful social reconnection every day. Write a positive e-mail to someone, put a card in the mail (remember snail mail and stamps?), Facebook someone in a positive way. Or pick up the phone and call someone to encourage them. Not a "woe is me" connection.

You Move in the Direction of Your Most Dominant Thoughts!

This is my second favorite saying. If you are thinking in a particular direction, you will move into that direction. No matter what it is! You believe what you say about yourself, even more than what *others* say about you. I know people who are always tired and run-down. They are constantly saying, "I'm so tired. I just don't have any energy, I'm old." They talk about it for so long; it becomes reality. Do not verbalize it. You will believe what you say because your brain will follow your words. It's just the way our brains are wired!

A Story

There was a story about a great baseball player who starred as a pitcher for Houston Astros. He was an outgoing, energetic, likable young ballplayer who usually exudes a positive attitude. They built a stadium for this baseball player, and after they finished the stadium, he entered and walked out to the pitcher's mound of the ball field. His first words out of his mouth were "I'll never be able to pitch in this stadium." That season was his worst year of his entire career.

We get what we say. This can happen to so many of us every day. Our words are so powerful; what we prophesy becomes a reality. What we think we become. But what we think negatively should never be verbalized. Once you verbalize it, you will believe it. That is just the way the brain works! Keep it to yourself and zip the negative words and say what you want to believe, even if you don't yet believe. Make the dominant thoughts positive and reflect what you want; then you will naturally move in that direction. This is how our brains are wired. Our attitude should be think what we want and what we want should ultimately be what makes us happy.

Changing our attitude is difficult because change is difficult. It means repeating it twenty-one times to create that habit in the brain. Don't talk about the way you are. Talk about the way you want to be. When you do that, it will not only change the way you feel, but also it will change your attitude.

You are one of a kind, a masterpiece, and when you look in the mirror, don't say "Oh, look at those wrinkles." Say "Good morning, you gorgeous thing." Speak and think positive, and that is what you will gravitate toward naturally.

When I was learning to play drums at age fifty, I had to learn to separate my hand movements from my foot movements. The kick drum with my right foot would need to be constant or a specific pattern, while my right hand would be a different pattern and the left hand to be even a different pattern alternating. My brain would naturally want to keep the right foot and right hand the same. The brain cannot separate these without repetition to switch the receptors in the brain. This repetitive movement would create new brain pathways and muscle memory, ultimately making it possible to separate drum patterns. Likewise, our brains will follow a thought process and cannot separate reality unless we condition it. For example, if we constantly verbalize the negative, through repetition the brain will remember. Similar to a computer, it stores lots of information, and what we input into the computer is what the computer will accept without regard to reality and will replay that information. When we go to retrieve the information, we will get exactly what we input into the computer in return. Garbage in, garbage out—so to speak. Our brains are computers, and our attitude is the information we are installing. What we think, we become. What we think continuously about is the direction we will go because we follow what we think about. Happiness is an attitude we make happen by repeated patterns and habits that bring about what we want.

A Story

I heard a story about two farmers. When the rain fell, one farmer said, "Thank you, Lord for watering our crops." But the other farmer said, "Yeah, but if the rain keeps up, it's going to rot the roots." When the sun came out, the positive farmer said, "Thank you, Lord, that our crops are getting the vitamins and minerals they need. We'll have a wonderful harvest this year." But the negative farmer said, "Yeah, but if it keeps up, it's going to scorch those plants. We're never going to make a living."

Don't we all know people who always focus on the negative? Make sure to guard against their negative attitudes. Don't let them infect your thinking! Stay focused on the positive things in life. It's so easy to slip into assuming the worst in life. Don't let your imagination run wild.

Don't allow those negative imaginations to play destructive games with you. It's very stressful to go around with a nagging, negative feeling, always thinking that something is wrong or could maybe go wrong.

Live by faith, not by fear. Many times you will sabotage yourself with negative imagination of the worst-case scenario. When you do that, negative things will come to pass, because that is what you are dwelling on. That is a self-fulfilling prophecy. What you think, you become.

Your brain is a computer, so don't even input the information into your brain.

If a person receives a bad report from the doctor, they've practically planned their own funeral by the end of the day. If the business has been slow, they are certain they'll be the first one to get laid off. Rather than discipline their thought life, they panic and always find themselves defeated, failing, struggling, and worrying. How can you even move on to better things in life if you are always thinking "It will never work out" or "It will never be good for me" or "I will never get ahead." Murphy's law is dead! Fear and faith both have the same thing in common. Both are believing in an unknown that has not yet happened.

Enthusiasm

When I was young, I was very enthusiastic but I was always called hyper by my family, aunts, uncles, and most adults. They began squelching this enthusiasm without realizing it. What they recognized and identified as hyper was more enthusiasm than hyperactivity.

I could always find an optimistic side of any situation, and I would run with any optimistic but calculated idea I had. Looking back, most of us can remember as children being more open and optimistic, less afraid of judgment. But as we become adults and life becomes ritualistic and sometimes dull, with many difficulties along the way, we lose our enthusiasm. We stop being creative and being productive, afraid of negative critics who will sabotage our efforts or, worse, judge us. Even judging our ideas subtly can wane our enthusiasm.

Does a little voice in your head sometimes sabotage your best efforts? When you habitually judge yourself, you erode your capacity for self-compassion, which research shows is critical for happiness. One trick to help you tune out negative noise is keep cheerful company. Many people trace that negative inner critic to the voices of pessimistic people they grew up with, says physician Susan Biali, MD, the author of *Live a Life You Love*. So spend as much time with upbeat people as you can. Optimism is a learned skill. Even the most hard-core person can become a happy-go-lucky individual. Optimism goes hand in hand with enthusiasm. Optimism is a choice. It is learned by how we practice thinking. Enthusiasm is a natural personality trait. You either have it or you don't. If it is squelched in the early years, it will not be as dominant. I lost my enthusiasm for life for the final few years in my real estate career. This was as a result of a crumbling thirty-year marriage and the real estate market collapsing and starting to show its ugly head, coupled with the attitude of people and their unrealistic expectations. The economy was affecting the demeanor of the general public, and I saw the writing on the wall. People were becoming very pessimistic. It seemed nothing was ever enough. My plan was to retire by 2010, but the harder I tried, the more the client demanded of me or the job demanded. Short sales were my specialty. Helping individuals negotiate with the bank before a short sale became a common word in real estate back in 2006 to 2009. I was living with my husband at the time I decided to retire. My husband would be described as a natural-born pessimist by most who would meet him. I became very efficient at ignoring pessimism, but eventually after thirty years, I needed a break. After I finally retired completely from real estate in 2011, a year later than I had anticipated, I was able to retire with a healthy nest egg. I spent lots of time meditating after I separated from my husband of thirty-three years in 2012. It was a trial separation that could go either way, and it was uncertain when I left exactly how permanent it would be. Fortunately I moved into one of our rental properties that came available after our tenant stopped paying rent and I had evicted them. In my new surroundings, I finally had hours of quiet time. Having no TV and no radio was such a refreshing atmosphere. My husband was raised with older parents that were fear based and lived by worse-case scenarios in a critical, negative, argumentative atmosphere. As we age, our tendencies, due to our formative years, become more prevalent and extremely exaggerated. Many times this causes disorders in later life such as oppositional defiant disorder. We become very good at pushing away feelings or covering them up using music, television, or puttering to cope with the negative self-talk that we have grown up with. Those negative destructive words creep back into our heads as we age if we don't pay attention and stop them instantly. I have studied behavior in my psychology textbook about the idea that anyone who needs continuous noise with no quiet time is most likely burying their private thoughts and can't bear to hear the self-talk in the silence because it is probably negative. They cover it up to protect themselves from themselves. It's a textbook mental disorder. That negative critical voice that you were raised around becomes a tape recording that continues to play in your head if it is not turned off. Instead of turning it off consciously, an individual will cover it up with continuous noise and achieve the same outcome of turning it off by covering it up. The problem with that is other individuals around them cannot escape the constant noise and cannot have *positive* self-talk because there is no gap of quiet. Unfortunately the noise is the TV full of murder or suicide or scandal and other negative noise.

I began to see the light at the end of the tunnel during this time alone. Just nine months and I began to feel happiness again. It took almost a year to get my sense of humor back. Many years of built-up resentment and anger began to subside for the first time in years.

I reflected on the many conversations I had with women when I did their nails every week during the nine years I owned my nail salon. Clients would complain about different parts of their lives and the feeling of being overwhelmed and unappreciated. This was true whether they were wealthy or poor, gorgeous or homely. This was many years ago, and I wondered if things had changed or if it was even more intense now with the economy so different and our standards of living becoming less disciplined. To find out, I began having deep conversations with many women during the course of a year. I discovered that their lives had only become more complex and complicated. I compiled a list of valid ideas on what women need and want. Menopause can be hard enough to control, compounded with no direction of how to be happy at fifty plus. I created the following chapters from my understanding of women and what they want and need at fifty plus. These twelve chapters will be individually looked at with new ideas and a different outlook to run your own race. Here is what I found about women at age fifty plus!

1. Women want to look back at their lives and be proud, but often are disappointed about their lives and feel like they are now going in circles.

2. Women are mostly the readers of self-help books and are more open to improvement and change than men.

3. Women use food to cope.

4. Women use alcohol or pot to cope and reminisce about the good old days.

5. Women need structure, but also need to learn how to relax and not feel guilty about a decision to be happy.

6. Women use divorce for a search to find happiness.

7. Women want to look pretty but don't know how.

8. Women become less tolerant at fifty plus.

9. Women need more time and more peace in this fast-paced world.

10. Women need to ignore what they can't control and embrace menopause.

11. Women need to make better decisions, depending on no one and practice happiness.

12. Women don't grasp their importance in the lives of their husbands, children, and all their relationships.

I have titled each chapter after the twelve areas I have found women want and need. I have researched from many authors on each subject, formed analogies to make it more clearly understood (you'll find I use lots of car analogies), and compiled what I have seen demonstrated and have experienced personally. I have studied philosophy in counseling and have a master's degree in counseling, which I received in 2009. I have never taken the opportunity for a counseling practice seriously until I was offered a position for a Tacoma center called Oasis of Hope Center. This position offers mental health care at no cost or low cost for individuals, couples, and families. When I owned a nail salon for over ten years, I was holding hands every week with many women of all ages. While doing their nails, they tell you everything. They open their heart to you. I clearly understand some of the frustrations women endure and the journey that many women travel to find happiness. As we move toward our sixties and to attain a sense of well-being and happiness, the results can be changed by the decisions we make and the state of mind we maintain while we are in our fifties. It can be a domino effect, each thing falling apart causing another fall, then another. We can learn how to listen to our inner voice when we think we should do something or not do something. Maybe a thought to slow down just before driving by a police car who has his radar gun on you or the funny feeling you get before making a decision to make a purchase that later turned out badly or a feeling you can't explain about calling your child or taking a different way home only later to see a wreck on the very street you would have traveled. It is imperative for you to open your mind to accept new ideas in order to have a direction change. "You must acknowledge a problem, before you can fix a problem."

Moving through these twelve common needs that women may have and not even recognize will bring us closer to the happiness that we desire and deserve at fifty plus. Hopefully you will learn how to practice happiness, and how practice makes perfect, so you will achieve happiness.

Women Look Back
at Their Lives

We can't change the past, as the past is just that. It is easy to be caught up remembering things that have been a disappointment. Maybe a divorce or a child whom you thought had great promise but was caught up in bad behavior, or a business that failed. You are not dead yet, and all of the past experiences may have been to direct you in the future to a better idea or experience or friendship that will bring about a new direction now. We move in the direction of our most dominant thoughts, so don't let the memories of the past corrupt your future by making them the dominant thought. There is always a bigger idea out there, but you must look for it. You don't know it because you only know what you have experienced up to the present. Who would have thought reality TV would be such a great success, spying on people's personal lives. Somebody had a vision and went for it! Shows like *Survivor*, *Big Brother*, *The Kardashians*, and *Housewives of* (every city you can think of). But here's an example of how a lack of ambitious vision could keep you from getting somewhere because we unknowingly sabotage ourselves.

A Story

There is a story about a little frog. This frog lived in a small pond and was perfectly happy in the pond. He grew up in the pond. One day he wanted to venture out to see what was beyond the pond that had been his home and where had become so comfortable in his whole life. He wandered away only to find a huge lake that was amazing! He could swim for miles before reaching the other side. He was so excited! He then thought after a while, *I wonder what is out there beyond this amazing lake.* He ventured out farther only to come to the largest pool of water he had ever imagined. It was the ocean. He was absolutely amazed at the enormous size. Now looking back, he was perfectly content for all of his life in the pond. If he had never ventured out, he would have been perfectly content. But if he had not ventured out, he would not have known about the lake. He was perfectly happy in his lake home, venturing farther only to find something as magnificent as the ocean.

This example only shows that we can't know what is beyond because we have not yet experienced it. We have a great opportunity to tap into the unknown, but we must be willing to venture out. Fear of the unknown because of our past disappointments could be what is holding you back. Just like the frog, you must be open to venture out and move in a direction that can be scary and uncomfortable.

If you have been a wife and/or a mother, you have accomplished a great task. We all know what is involved in doing a great job of raising a child and being an accommodating wife. You may have done everything right in your own mind, but things still may not have turned out as you may have hoped. Be proud of who you have become and who you have been in the past. We all have made mistakes, bad decisions, and have regrets, but if we learn from them, they have not been a waste of time or tears. Many times it is not just one bad decision but a domino effect of several decisions. A later chapter will discuss a method to making good decisions.

Make an effort to enlarge your circle of friends now that you are fifty plus. Others are feeling the same and reflecting on their lives as well. You are not the only one with regrets and past mistakes. This is the time to begin connecting with other positive individuals who share your same feelings and disappointments. These friends, who you connect with or reconnect with, will be your strength when you are far into your seventies. Don't let the past infect your attitude and potential for the future.

Embrace the past as the stepping stone to the future.

Be a Person of Excellence

A person of excellence is someone who goes the extra mile. Someone who takes the time to bend over to pick up a piece of trash in the walkway. Not able to be slothful. Has social grace and does the right thing even if it is not the popular thing. A person of excellence can be empathetic because it is easy to put themselves in others' shoes instantly and acknowledge another's circumstances with little or no judgment. A person of excellence is someone who honors others and gives them respect. This means you look for opportunities to compliment others or encourage them, not look for flaws first. Your attitude should be, Who can I make feel better today? Who can I put a good word in for? How can I make them feel special? If you get extra special service at a restaurant from someone, take the time to talk to the manager to let them know what a great job they did. A person of excellence will always look for ways to honor or bring others up. If you show honor to others, it will directly affect how much you will be blessed. The Bible tells us, "*Take delight in honoring one another.*" If you take the time to make others feel special regularly, it will become a habit. The kind words will always come back to you. Celebrate others who are being promoted. "Don't keep it to yourself. Send out a note to a friend, Facebook or text them. Call your parents and take the time for them. We are all busy! We are people of excellence. It's easy to be competitive and not want to give someone else a compliment. If someone is getting married and you are still single, don't be jealous. Honor them anyway. Don't miss opportunities to be good to others. Be generous with your compliments. Be stingy with your complaints. There is enough gossip, slander, talking behind other people's back. Put in a good word about somebody, it will get back to them, and a secondhand compliment can be more potent than you may realize. It's easy to find fault, but people of excellence are not faultfinders. "A person's harvest in life will depend entirely on what they sow" (Galatians

6). You can't sow dishonor to others and expect to have honor come back to you. A person of excellence is not dishonoring to their ex-spouse or their crazy brother at family gatherings. Protect your family and stand up for each other. Understand one another's circumstances with little or no judgment.

We produce what we continually keep in front of us. If we focus on an image of success, in your mind you're going to move toward success. If you see yourself as barely getting by, your marriage getting worse, your health going downhill, then most likely your life will gravitate toward those negative situations. Your vision, what you see, has a tremendous impact in your life. We need to quit allowing our imaginations to keep us beaten down, reflecting on the past. Instead start allowing yourself to use your imagination to build yourself up. Keep the goals you want to see in front of you, and that image will set the limits for your life. The old saying "Look out the car windshield in front of you, not your rearview mirror."

The following areas are a few major reflections on the past by which we judge ourselves. Let's look at a new approach to view them.

Marriage

I, myself, have experienced the process of a divorce, moving toward ending a thirty-three-year marriage to my first love. I had to come to a conclusion to why I cannot fulfill my promise of "Till death do us part." I struggled with this for a very, very long time due to my upbringing and personal beliefs. I now can see how many women feel! They feel like they failed. "If I had only tried harder" or "If I had just learned to live with his ways." Although the papers for the dissolution of my marriage are completed, they have not been filed. Chapter 6 on marriage goes into great detail and will be helpful to bring about important changes in your relationship with your partner as you approach retirement. Techniques and questions in chapter 6 will be addressed to help you become more self-protective, more assertive, more effective, and less vulnerable to the manipulation, confusion, and sometimes loss of self-confidence. One basic conclusion about marriage is simple: There are a lot of girlfriends that I have known for many years and can be around for two hours or four hours or even all day. There are friends I could possibly stay at a hotel for the weekend and enjoy their company, but I could never live with any of my friends twenty-four hours a day every day for the rest of my life! That's it in a nutshell. When it comes to a long-term marriage, it becomes too familiar, which causes complacency. Living together every day while raising kids or grandkids, so much emotional baggage has built up, and as time goes by, women begin to change and grow. Many times women reinvent themselves at different rates and in different directions during the course of a long marriage.

Many may assume that I have a perfect marriage. Many who know me well enough know that it is far from the case, but perfection in marriage is simply not even possible. It would seem hypocritical for me to even counsel couples who have marriage difficulties. But actually I have learned firsthand games that are played, and studied manipulation and mental disorders for years during my marriage. What would be better than someone who has lived it, not just read about it? We are human. Lots of physicians get sick, models gain weight and get zits, and brilliant engineers build bridges that crack and collapse too. Though I would like to believe that I could blame my husband by thinking, "If he would just shape up we could have a better marriage," but I must confess to making a sizable contribution to an imperfect relationship. Not always deliberately, but the result is still the same: disappointment on both sides. Most of us have to work very hard to keep a relationship rewarding to both parties. There have been times my husband and I have argued all the way to a party, all the way to the door before ringing the doorbell then happily smiling, looking calm and pleasant all through cocktails and dinner, actually enjoying ourselves. Then after the good-byes to our host and hostesses resuming our hostilities on our way back to the car. I believe this is typical of lots of marriages, but thank goodness not too often. It is the same as dealing with a cold or flu. Now and then you get it. You feel feverish and rotten, but you work at taking care of yourself, and you soon recover. You would never *want* it, but it is unavoidable and part of a marriage. Marriage is probably the biggest challenge we face in life. In my opinion it needs more thought, care, attention, and energy than most other jobs we take on. *Jobs* sounds suspiciously like work. Most of us went into marriage with the expectation that it would be fun that *followed* hard work, not more hard work in itself! We were disillusioned and now must come to terms with it. If you had worked hard to take good care of your marriage in the first place, you would not be feeling this discomfort. Is Marriage for everyone? Not in a million years. Some people should avoid it like the plague. Those who put a high priority on independence and autonomy might never be willing to pay the price of constantly working together. Society has made marriage almost a given for so long, and unfortunately lots of people choose marriage because they think it's expected of them. It is becoming less true today as we see more singles living alone than ever before. I am happy to see we are coming to see marriage as an option rather than a necessity.

My husband had retired at fifty-three in 2001. Now I was retiring and home much more, just playing drums in two bands on weekends and several weekly rehearsals. My counseling practice at Oasis of Hope Center in Tacoma was three days a week, allowing me my own flexible schedule. Now you add to the mix a new lifestyle, late-night schedules, and different agenda and expectations for retirement to that scenario and guess what happens? You've grown and changed, and so has your spouse. Sometimes without realizing it, you have unintentionally disconnected from your spouse while deeply focused on working hard at your job or career. This allowed you to wander in separate directions. After kids and careers, you look at this spouse many years later and say "I love being with you, but I can't live with you 24/7 for the rest of my life." Some of you who are divorced already understand this perfectly. Having felt this personally for the first time while being separated, I have had time to reflect and acknowledge this fact. If you are getting close to retiring and your spouse is already retired, be very cognizant of this new adapting you will have to embrace. You have the right to be you, and so does your spouse when you retire. How dare anyone say you must be like you *used to be*! What? Do you mean when I was twenty-three years old? That would be unrealistic and frankly crazy and very scary if you were exactly the same person in every way at age fifty something as you were at age twenty-three! We must grow, just like flowers and plants. How much we were watered and loved along the way is a huge factor for our growth. How we behave and how we feel about ourselves now is a reflection quite often to how much our *spouse* watered us and how much *we* watered our spouse. When we are ready to retire and be with this spouse all day, it will come to light and be very evident. Happiness will be decided by some major factors.

Men marry women, hoping they stay the same. Women marry men, hoping they will change.

Unfortunately neither happens. Women don't stay the same. They tend to grow and change. Likewise, men don't change. They stay very much as creatures of habit and are unassuming and consistent.

Women can be likened to delicate plants. Water, not poison, contributes to growth. I perceive compliments as water. This water (compliment) would be poured on us, as if it were water on a beautiful plant. We women are this beautiful plant! Other relationship virtues such as helpfulness, diligence, being supportive, or anything else that a woman needs to flourish can be classified as water. Compliments are extremely underrated. But many of us have not had a lot of watering (compliments). We have had lots of poison poured on us. Swearing, condescending attitude, hurtful ridiculing, and judgmental directing, even during an argument is verbal poison. This can do so much harm to an individual's soul and spirit. Condescending attitudes, continuous ridiculing, and controlling another's thoughts and actions are like poison. We unknowingly allow this drought and pouring of poison to continue due to being young and inexperienced, not being a confrontational person, or it began so subtly we were oblivious to it, or a combination of all three. Women many times allow the behavior to continue many years into retirement. Slowly withering away with no watering and only poison until we die inside.

This is why the best decision you may have made was to end the marriage—if that is what you did or are possibly planning to do. Maybe this book will let you see areas you can watch out for in your future relationships. It could also possibly challenge your thinking, allowing your perspective on things to change radically, and your marriage could become better than ever for your retirement years. Using specific questions for defining what you want and setting limits for your relationship should be considered before making a decision of divorce. Divorce should be for the right reasons. The right reason, clearly, is to be happy for your remaining years. If you are fortunate enough to have a happy, compatible marriage, then you will continue to grow together and be happy. However, as time goes on, there are many things you should be aware of and watch out for to keep the growth and direction moving toward happiness and not fall into destructive patterns or tolerate bad behavior for your future retirement years. A chapter later in the book will talk about how we as women will tolerate a lot of grief. God designed women to be tenacious, strong spirited, and to have a natural desire to have companionship. A woman will not naturally give up on the marriage after the vows are taken in 97 percent of the cases. A woman dreams from the time she is a little girl of having a wedding and a husband and maybe children and a house with a white picket fence. This is not how it always works out, however. Many times we unknowingly do unrepairable damage in the first few years of marriage. At retirement, we improperly address unresolved issues that surface like a volcano. Most of us enter marriage with an unspoken contract, so to speak, and most of us assume that our spouse-to-be has the same contract in their mind. The contract most of us had in mind when we marry reads something like this:

Contract

1. I hereby agree to give you all the power in my life.

2. I renounce the right to make myself happy, knowing that from now on it is up to you to do it for me.

3. I will look to *you* for all my companionship, instead of having additional friends in my life.

4. Every need I now have, I expect you to fill.

5. In exchange, I will try to fill *your* every need. This gives me the right to advise and control you, because I know what is best for you.

6. With our responsibility for each other, we must match each other's mood. If you are angry or sad, I will be angry or sad too. One must never be happy unless both are happy.

7. Because you are the most important person in my life, should I ever be unhappy, it will clearly be your fault; and it is therefore your responsibility to try to reverse my mood.

8. Our signatures on this contract negate any responsibility for our individual selves that we might previously have held.

Signed _____and_____

I am reasonably sure none of us would have signed this contract if it was presented to us in this manner before the wedding. Yet foolishly many of us expect marriage to "make us happy."

The decision to make the marriage work or ending the marriage is never taken lightly by any woman I have ever known. Regrets of divorcing at this point are wasted energy. Learning from decisions that may or may not have been the right decision simply gives us new opportunity and insight for our future decisions.

I polished a lot of fingernails sitting at my nail table while they told me in detail how difficult it was to make the decision of divorce. Many boxes of Kleenex ruined freshly polished nails for those women who decided to end their marriage. Not once in hundreds, maybe thousands, of women were they not deeply hurting.

Whether we are married now or single, we can now move forward with the decisions we have already made at this point and good decisions needing to be made in the future. We can relax and learn about ourselves as we look at what will make us happy in our fifties, and you run your own race.

Excess Baggage

I've always loved the saying "I don't *need* a man, I choose a man!" What do you do with excess baggage? You get rid of it. At the airport they charge you for baggage, and if you don't need it, you surely wouldn't pay $25 for it! But if you are toting around an enormous amount of life and its responsibilities, emotional baggage, and completely carrying your partner's load, who has nothing but contempt for you, it may be time to rethink what is fair to yourself and most likely your partner. This doesn't mean you expect to be happy all the time when you are married. Every little squabble over taking out the garbage or responsibility is up for negotiation. If you aren't happy carrying all the baggage, his and yours, chances are your partner isn't very happy hearing you comment or complain about it. Sometimes familiarity breeds contempt. This was spoken to me by a bass player in my band, Lawrence, at a rehearsal one day and it stuck in my mind for a while. I realized it is very true. If you are with someone all the time for a long period of time and you read the definition of *contempt*, you might believe that innocently and unintentionally you could begin to feel this way when you are so comfortable being with each other.

Contempt [noun] 1. The feeling with which a person regards anything considered mean, vile, or worthless; disdain; scorn. 2. The state of being despised; dishonor; disgrace. 3. A feeling that a person or thing is beneath one's dignity and unworthy of one's notice, respect, or concern

I have an analogy I like to use for excess baggage. Imagine two large flat dinner plates that hold slippery spaghetti noodles. One is your partner's plate, and one is your plate. When you are first married and everything is new and wonderful, you divide the spaghetti noodles (which represent responsibilities and life's baggage) on the plates fairly evenly with tasks of bill paying, child care responsibilities, household chores, washing cars, doctor's appointments, shopping, cooking, meal planning, financial planning, vacation planning, household maintenance, etc., etc., etc. After some time you see your plates begin to get fuller as more things come into your lives. You purchase new furniture, new cars, have children, and so on. These noodles are slippery, and you are struggling to keep them in the center of the plate. You grow and change year after year. Then you notice your partner scrapping a few more spaghetti noodles (responsibility) onto your plate, which is now beginning to spill over. Your partner's plate now has five little noodles on it, and you are struggling to keep it all in a pile on your own plate without any falling off. You may try to scrape some back over onto your partner's plate, but that only lasts for a moment, and before long, they are scraping it back onto your already overflowing plate of noodles.

This is what is considered excess baggage. No one is happy doing it all in a partnership—a partnership in marriage, partnership in a business, or even in a rock 'n' roll band. Tasks and responsibilities should be shared. Positive, considerate people share the load. That is the problem with our society and our government today. Nobody wants to take the responsibility or ownership of anything they do or don't do. If you don't have a partnership of sharing the load in your life, it is time to find it and find it fast so you can allow yourself to be happy and relaxed. But you can't have it both ways. If you want to share the load equally, you must accept the idea of continuing conversation, compromise, negotiation, and respectful communication for the life of the marriage. Consider this in your life. Look at your life and see how full your plate is and maybe it is time to start scraping it back onto someone else's plate. If it isn't divided evenly or has now ended up all on your plate, you can make a nonnegotiable plate scraping. You don't want to retire from your career at work to take on a career of being a stellar maid, cook, problem solver, and planner do you? This will suck up your energy and your time, leaving no time to enjoy your retirement.

An entire chapter is dedicated to divorce, but in this introduction section of marriage, I must point out the standard of practice! Standard of practice for realtors is defined very clearly from a legal standpoint and was put in place to keep people from taking advantage of a situation or being unfair. This code of ethics could come in handy in the division of property and assets in a marriage that is ending. It could be used as a guideline for how to treat our soon to be ex-spouses as well. This is just a section of the code that was written in 2012:

Code of Ethics for Realtors

Code of Ethics and Standards of Practice of the NATIONAL ASSOCIATION OF REALTORS ®

Effective January 1, 2012

Realizing that cooperation with other real estate professionals promotes the best interests of those who utilize their services, REALTORS® urge exclusive representation of clients; do not attempt to gain any unfair advantage over their competitors; and they refrain from making unsolicited comments about other practitioners. In instances where their opinion is sought, or where REALTORS® believe that comment is necessary, their opinion is offered in an objective, professional manner, uninfluenced by any personal motivation or potential advantage or gain.

Now—let's exchange the word 'Realtor' for the word 'Partner' (whom you may be divorcing) and apply this to our behavior during a divorce. Most of us consider ourselves to have good ethics…but actions speak louder than words.

Code of Ethics for Divorcing Individuals

Realizing that cooperation with the other partner promotes the best interests of both parties. Do not attempt to gain any unfair advantage over the other partner and refrain from making unsolicited comments about the other partner. In instances where their opinion is sought, or where the other partner would believe that comment is necessary, the opinion is offered in an objective, professional manner, uninfluenced by any personal motivation or potential advantage or gain.

This is easier said than done, but if we use this standard of practice during the marriage dissolution, we can treat the division as if we are dividing with a friend whom we have an amicable separation. Imagine how much less hurt we would have during a divorce. Our children would have less negative effect from a divorce, not to mention less turmoil and stress for everybody involved. That would also be the best way to eliminate any guilt. Someone who feels guilty about screwing the other partner over is less likely to forgive themselves. People who don't forgive themselves are not much fun to be around. Guilt-ridden people are not very happy people. You use the standard of practice as your guide regardless of what the other partner is using. Let the other person involved feel guilty and be unhappy! Don't allow others to influence your ethic and standard of practice. You run your own race. My divorce decree has been completed and remains unsigned at the present, but it has a standard of practice for every section. Others with good intentions are always quick to offer advice or opinions based on their experience dealing with divorce, but ignoring others and doing what feels right to you as an individual is how you run your own race.

Let's talk about sex and why I'd rather go to sleep. Okay, I admit after four very intense demanding careers, a child I raised, and thirty-plus years of marriage, it's not easy to get in the mood for sex. Men disagree. Men have the ability to be in the mood no matter what the situation is. Many women would have to admit that often we prefer a great night of sleep to an orgasm. I kept thinking once I get caught up on sleep, we were retired. It would be the two of us in the house. We would both be in the mood at the same time. Well, nobody warned me that menopause would get in the way. Marriages have seasons. And it is fun to be sexy sometimes, but there is a peace in accepting we are past the "star-spangled banner"—period. Sure, hotels are fun because it renews the spark and the faith that we want to be together. Things ebb and flow, and during the ebb times, love and passion manifest itself in different little ways, like sharing morning coffee and paper, taking a walk on a windy day hand in hand. So don't get discouraged and give up because you may not be as frisky as you used to be and maybe your husband would like you to initiate things more often. If you both are determined to make it better, then that is all that matters.

Speaking about men wanting more initiation brings up another fear women have in their marriage: infidelity. An article written recently described the degree of effort and difficulty it is for a man to even have the time or the desire to part with the money for any outside activity with another woman, much less a relationship. It's easy to wonder since you see politicians, movie stars, CEOs, and athletes make the news due to infidelity. Have American husbands lost their moral compass? Probably not. Men disingenuously identify themselves as hunters, as opposed to gatherers; thus, this deems them biologically incapable of remaining monogamous. This rationalization is not for all men. Men will justify infidelity by believing and thinking their wives *no longer love them. The sex fell off after kids were born,* they would say, or *the thrill is gone.* When they are brutally honest, they might come clean that they found a younger woman—someone with a better body, richer, awesome sex. Men can be pigs! But most are not. Statistics show that cheating is not nearly as rampant with ordinary men as it may seem in the jock world or high-octane suites. According to the General Social Survey conducted by the National Opinion Research Center at the University of Chicago, no more than 22 percent of men have ever engaged in marital infidelity, and only one man in twenty is unfaithful to his wife on an annual basis. So if a man calls his wife and tells her he is working late, there is a 95 percent chance that he's stuck in his chair working hard, not cheating. Men are more likely to stray than women— or at least more likely to admit it. The gender gap is closing; however, a new study shows nearly 15 percent of women say they have cheated.

Faithful men adore their wives even if things are not always blissful. But is it possible that these husbands refrain from cheating not so much because they love their wives, and not even because they view cheating as immoral, but for other reasons? Why some men are faithful to their wives may give you some assurance that your average man is safe from worry.

- *Men are incredibly lazy.* Men like to plop down on the couch and watch sports and drink beer. Romance would be labor intensive and would require a shower, shave, some deodorant, putting on something other than sweatpants, buying flowers, going to the movies, reading a book every once in a while, engaging in conversation, and thinking of compliments. Cheating on your wife would involve dinner reservations, sometimes travel, and booking hotels. To a married man that is just *way* too much energy and could be exhausting. Need I say more!

- *Men are starting to get ugly.* Women may say looks are not as important to them and a good sense of humor is more important. But if you look around, you may see a 10 with an 8, or an 8 with a 5, but rarely do you see a 9 with a 2.

Ugly men don't cheat because they are grateful to have someone and would never risk it.

- *Men are cheap.* Having an extramarital affair takes money. Even if it does not involve elaborate trips, sooner or later you will have to shell out some dough for a meal.

- *Men fear getting caught.* Six percent of men in America view cheating as acceptable. Sixty-four percent say it is unforgivable. The risk of getting caught is enormous. A simple charge on a Visa could be a mistake with consequences.

- *Men don't have extra time.* There are barely enough hours in the day to maintain a happy marriage let alone an extramarital affair. At a certain point, having a mistress is just another job.

- *Men have seen* Fatal Attraction. Need any more be said!

So now you can rest assured that there are millions and millions of faithful men who cherish and love their wives and would never be unfaithful. But being faithful in a marriage is not always the direct result of an iron-clad value system; however, I would like to believe that it is.

Marriage is not when one person *rules* another. It is based on a mutual respectful relationship, and the submissive one is almost sure to rebel somewhere along the way.

Weight Gain

We struggle on managing our weight our whole lives to some degree, but never as much as when we are older. Fifty plus is a challenge due to many factors. Obviously hormones changing the way we metabolize food, as well as stress, which produces more cortisol, making us store fat as a natural protection. But we can change what we put into our bodies to offset those unchangeable factors to some degree. A recent book written by J. J. Virgin called the *Virgin Diet* was an interesting theory to consider. A close friend of mine, Cheri, who is extremely disciplined by nature, recently really struggled with weight gain since her unemployment. She began following this diet. At the very least, it taught her the importance of certain foods and the values and nutritional combinations of many foods. She was very successful with completing this diet and follows it for much of her everyday food choices, as a result maintaining her weight. It essentially removes from your diet seven items for three weeks and slowly introduces them back into your body. This system helps you pay close attention to your reaction as you are completely free of these items in your system. You then slowly reintroduce them after three weeks (if you stuck to the program). This is what is done for testing the reaction to gluten and testing for allergies.

Sugar is a big accelerant to aging, which is a fact. Sugar also triggers fat storage as well as does fructose. So this is not a surprise that removing sugar is one of the major items. The additional items to remove in no particular order: soy, eggs, corn, peanuts, dairy, gluten, and sugar. Sugar being your biggest enemy. These items are a lot of our staple foods. But if you feel like trying something different, read her book and give it an attempt because it isn't unhealthy. She is an advocate for grass-fed cows and other animals as well as vegetable and fruit intake every day. Exchanging peanuts with walnuts and almonds is not a huge switch (just more expensive). Corn is not a vegetable, which I have always believed. Our chips are from corn, our tortillas, and many other products are corn based, so eliminating them in your diet is a tough task. If you take the time at the store to look at the main ingredients, you will be shocked at what products have corn in it.

There are a million types of diets. We all crave instruction so choosing one diet or a combination can be a challenge, keeping in mind the good old days when food was less processed and modified. This means less packaged foods and requiring us to cook more. Organic...maybe...but I have lived by an acronym that has kept me on track every day for many years, and it works for me. I feel better because of it. I am not advocating any one particular diet and certainly not a fan of the vegan diet. I've seen the vegan diet ruin too many people's lives, sabotaging them terribly while under the assumption that it is healthy.

We are the size we are right now. Let's accept that, first of all. We can wish we were a different size, but starting from wherever we are, it's important to find an eating lifestyle with food restrictions we can live with! That is the whole trick, it just makes sense.

Here an acronym I live by:

GOMBS, like combs but with a *G*. It's easy! Each day eat a small amount of each of these!

- G = Greens
- O = Onions
- M = Mushrooms
- B = Beans and Berries
- S = Seeds

That's it...every day! I try hard to include a portion of each one of these every day. Some days are better than others. Take a multivitamin. Also include calcium and vitamin D daily (especially if you live in Washington State where there is less sunshine for vitamin D absorption).

Notice there is no meat, dairy, or bread in there. Meat, dairy, and bread are side dishes. Just that small change in thinking can make a huge difference! A salad for lunch can include a bunch of these GOMBS right off the bat—adding tomatoes, sprouts, some kidney beans from a can, saltine crackers, and walnuts, and POW! Think of meat as a side dish rather than a main dish. By making meat a side dish, you create interesting meals using vegetables you enjoy.

I am not a diet expert, but as an aerobics dance instructor in 1984 to 1995, as well as performing in a dance company for many years, I relied on good protein as fuel and studied in great detail the use and needs of our bodies. I learned how to utilize the most efficient combination of foods to maximize my efforts. I think balance again seems to be the key. I remember when I was teaching eleven classes of aerobic dance every week in the 1980s, I created handout flyers each month that I would give to eighty women who took my aerobic dance classes. I would cut out recipes, ideas, tricks for good healthy eating and living, and paste them on a piece of paper in a collage format and copy them on a Xerox machine (remember those machines?) I would hand them out at the beginning of each month before the classes. That is how much I believed in diet and how intake along with activity plays hand in hand on balance and weight management. We must take care of our bodies. We are only given one body with no backup. This is it. You wreck it, you own it wrecked!

I am a total lover of Jarlsberg swiss cheese. It is one of the only cheeses that one slice can actually help guard against lung cancer. (Dr. Oz discussed this.) It comes in reduced fat and is a swiss cheese with nine grams of protein and a lot less fat. If you are a cheese lover, then switch to this cheese. Also feta cheese comes in low fat or fat free and great for spinach salad with walnuts. (Watch out, sometimes fat free can have more sugar). Be especially careful with yogurt that is fat free. It contains lots of sugar, so compare each brand for plain yogurt.

Super Foods That Power You Up

- Blueberries—God's candy, ranks among the top disease-fighting foods

- Avocados—God's mayonnaise, improves overall hormone function
- Basil/Mint—God's herbs, used for thousands of years in Chinese medicine for digestion and inflammation
- Olives/Olive oil—Lowers blood pressure and cholesterol
- Walnuts—Twice as many antioxidants as other nuts
- Wild Salmon—God's fish, omega 3 fatty acids, helps prevent aging
- Coffee—Loaded with antioxidants, helps cell damage, reduce disease
- Thyme—Fights bacteria, treats acne
- Kale—Rich in vitamin K, has triple lutein in one serving than raw spinach, helps with sleep disorders and insomnia
- Green Tea—Antioxidant to protect cells, cancers
- Sweet Potatoes—Vitamin B6 and potassium
- Dark Chocolate—Aids in decreasing blood pressure and cholesterol
- Asparagus—God's bamboo, diuretic, high in potassium, vitamin B12, repairs cells.
- Pomegranates—Keep cardiovascular healthy
- Garlic—When crushed releases allicin, which wards off heart attacks and strokes.

- Yogurt—Restores balance in gastrointestinal tract.

- Honey and cinnamon combined—Helps with arthritis, clearing arteries in heart and prevents strokes and much more.

I will address aspects of eating and habits and helpful ideas in future chapters. We need to remove our guilt for past diet failures. We must stand in the mirror with our clothes off and ask, "Is this what I want?" If the answer is yes, then think healthy and keep moving forward in the same direction, keeping an open mind to new ideas and new findings as best you can. If the answer is no, then think healthy and move in a different direction. Research foods and diets on your own. You are worth the time! You know what will work for you and your personality and lifestyle. The old saying for the meaning of insanity is doing the same thing over and over and expecting a different result!

A couple of mottoes I have kept at the front of my brain when shopping for food is "*I eat what I buy, and I buy what I'll eat.*" This prevents waste of good healthy food but also pushes you to try new things. Second motto is "*I eat to live, not live to eat.*" Food should not be the most dominant thought on your mind all the time, aside from preparation or purchasing it. Retirement can allow you so much extra time that you unknowingly allow food to become your main focus every day.

Exploring Dopamine

Dopamine is very powerful. This chemical is created in our bodies, and I call it an instigator for addiction. Did you know that if you think about doing something you enjoy or like to do such as drink a cold beverage on a hot day or check your iPhone, the thought of that will light up an entire dopamine-driven reward pathway in your brain? It's true! You try but you can't get that urge out of your head. You give in. And then, as soon as you satisfy the raging urge, bingo. You feel another rush. Your brain says, "Yeah! This is amazing, I want more." You need your fix. For the most part, this neurological process can be a good thing. This same reward system drives us to learn, create, be innovative, and to pursue our goals. But a medical doctor, Pam Peeke, MD, MPH, who specializes in metabolism and weight management has discovered that a rush of dopamine—the brain chemical that makes us feel a brief burst of pleasure and satisfaction—cuts both ways. That healthy high you get from a run in the park occupies the same pathways as a dopamine hit from a snort of cocaine or a puff of a cigarette. Pam Peeke has discovered that the cries for help are similar to those of a hard-core drug or alcohol addict. "I need the sugar fix." "I'll go crazy with withdrawal." "I need a dose of pizza." "Chips and dip are like cocaine or crack to me. Once I start, I can't stop." These cravings are the result of a reward system gone awry. New science shows that the mere anticipation of a food-related dopamine high will cause the brain's reward centers to light up Times Square on New Year's Eve. When you understand this fact, you can prepare and act accordingly and tell yourself what you need to do different. Knowledge is power only if you use it. Dopamine equals pleasure, and we are human and crave pleasure. Being aware of this power Dopamine has will keep us choosing fruit for sugar instead of doughnuts. We will choose protein instead of a carbohydrate, which later converts to sugar anyway! Sugar acts like dopamine.

One of my clients I have been counseling at Oasis of Hope is a recovering methamphetamine addict. She recently left her long nine-year relationship with her boyfriend who was an addict. One thing I encouraged her to do is find her dopamine fix. She has had the drugs that her brain enjoyed so much, but she needed to explore activities and crafts that she would get the same high as the meth provided. This will put her in control. It also prevents exposure to something else to replace that high that may not be a good replacement. After talking a while, she remembered that she made cards from scratch going to Michael's and buying craft materials and really enjoyed doing it. She also loves music, and she and her brother would sing at the church together. She was thinking of getting back to that. She loves to go camping and will plan to go this summer. If you don't take the time to find your dopamine fix in this society of immediate gratification and constant search for enjoyment away from your troubles, something will pop up, and you will grab it. For some it would be smoking, for others it may be eating or drinking alcohol. There are lots of hobbies and skills that will bring about the same high. Take a minute to explore your personal dopamine fix. Everybody has one. Maybe one that is a secret?

Take a few minutes to write down a list of things that fire up your brain and excite you.

Do you see the dopamine circle?

see the Dopamine circle?

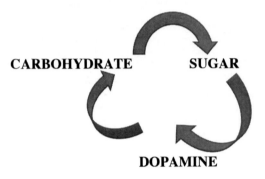

CARBOHYDRATE   **SUGAR**

DOPAMINE

Health

Starting with mental health, my OCD kicks in when it comes to my teeth. I am one of those people who will go to the trouble to put toothpaste on her string of floss and floss with toothpaste, scrubbing between each tooth, which makes a big mess by the way, and toothpaste gets all over your cheeks and your nose by the time you finish (not to mention, it makes a mess on your mirror!). I am driven to get a new toothbrush every couple weeks, can never go to bed *ever* without brushing my teeth. It never made sense to me to run a plain piece of waxed string between your teeth, yet we use toothpaste on the top and sides of the teeth! So this makes sense to me to use toothpaste on the floss. It is an obsessive thing I do along with putting baking soda in the palm of my hand and dabbing my toothbrush in it to scrub my teeth occasionally. Believe it or not, it actually brightens your teeth and helps keep them white. A trick I learned from my mother when I was young. However, she would add salt in the soda as well to scrub. How funny that we retain so much from our upbringing. I about gave the dental hygienist a heart attack when I told her I used salt. She said the salt is absorbed immediately into your body and not a good habit to indulge in. I guess for an obsession this is a better compulsion to have, resulting in lower dental bills.

If you are OCD about something or obsessive about something, pay attention to what it may be. Later in an upcoming chapter we talk about mental health and its impact on your physical health

Move More

Don't sit around every day. One day is absolutely fine. Everybody needs a day to veg out. But typically, if you tend to sit around a lot, you are sabotaging yourself. Studies show that sitting is why Americans are getting fatter. When you sit, your metabolism automatically slows down, so you begin to store fat. I challenge you to fill up your schedule at least four days during a seven-day week where you are out all day, or busy getting things done. Not sitting at any one time for more than an hour without moving for ten minutes. Park in the middle of the parking lot no matter where you go and walk at least two minutes to the destination store. If you work, do this for four days after work, or all day if you stay at home. Continue staying busy four days each week for a twenty-one-day stretch for six continuous weeks. Try exchanging sitting at home watching TV for an activity in the evening of some time at least four days every week. You are conditioning your body. You will notice you feel better and have a feeling of well-being with more energy after just six weeks.

For every one hour you sit, you need to move around or get up for ten minutes. People who fidget tend to be slimmer because they are in motion. Motion is the secret to long life. Exercise or gym time does not undo a whole day of sitting, unfortunately. This includes sitting in the office, at home, in a movie theater, or at a friend's house and even nighttime TV. Get up during commercials and empty the dishwasher. This is one reason I hate the Comcast and Dish TV ability to fast-forward through commercials of taped shows. You can't get a break to move or do something during commercials because you have efficiently scrolled through them. This feature comes in handy when you are trying to watch a taped show quickly but has its downfall of never allowing you to move and stretch in the evening. Just move more! That is why our gym time seems so futile. Not sitting for hours is a behavior you can change for your health. It takes discipline, but doable. I type on my typewriter sometimes standing up at the counter in my kitchen or in my drum room office at my bar for hours. I just discovered a new water sport called stand-up paddling. I tried it and loved it. I will be purchasing a paddleboard as soon as I can.

I am grateful I took up a musical instrument that demands high energy and lots of calorie consumption. Personally I would get bored standing and plucking on a guitar! But that is my personality, and you may be more easygoing and have a laid-back nature. Plan on struggling more in this first attempt to move more and stay in motion. It will get easier after it becomes a habit in twenty-one days. Move more for twenty-one days every day. Pretend you have hemorrhoids then you won't sit much. Try tennis, if you have played in the past. There are lots of empty outdoor tennis courts growing weeds from lack of use. Don't use the excuse of too much risk. That is what people say when they just don't want to move more! There is less risk in doing an activity on a regular basis than the risk of health issues and heart disease if you don't! Sixty years old is the new fifty, and fifty years old is the new forty. We are more active and knowledgeable than our parents about health and fitness, not to mention technology and social media.

I always feel better after playing drums at a show with the band on a weekend by doing something physical the next day like washing the car or washing the windows, painting a wall, gardening, or anything that makes me bend and move to stretch. It actually lengthens those muscles that were used in playing drums. Playing drums for four hours on Friday and many times four hours on Saturday make my muscles tighten, retract, and shorten. Stretching takes the soreness out. You must try it. If I sit on the couch all day after a gig, I feel more sore and miserable on the following day.

You may not be as healthy as you would like to have been in the past, or as active in the past, but why not start new habits. Make some small new habits, which only take twenty-one days to create and soon will feel like second nature and normal. You are in charge of your own health. Sometimes your head has to lead you, and then after you start doing the activity, your heart will lead the rest of the way. If you have ever been talked into doing something, you didn't want to do but you did it anyway, before long you really have a good time. Later wondering why you didn't want to do it. Lead with your head and your heart will follow. Many times when I am watching television I say to myself *I need to go work on my drums for a while.* My heart doesn't really feel like it at that particular time, but if I follow my head first, then after playing drums for a while my heart gets excited and I'm completely engaged and happy I decided to practice.

Moving more requires you to tell yourself what to do. What you practice you become good at!

Careers

This is an area of much regret. Men tend to derive their sense of accomplishment by their work or careers. But more and more women also base their self-esteem on their accomplishments in their careers. If we stopped working at a job to take care of our children through the early years of their growing before returning to work, we may have regrets. Our portfolio for retirement may reflect that loss of income during that time too. Perhaps we never returned to work due to reasons we felt were appropriate at the time. Regardless of our past, we can accomplish anything we want if we want it bad enough. The economy may be down, but small businesses are developing, and people are supporting the "little guy" more than ever. Many times I will stop at a small coffee shop rather than Starbucks just to support the small business.

If you have had your career and now must go back to work due to divorce or circumstances, then just make sure it will be a job you will enjoy. Don't choose to be unhappy by drudging through a day doing a job you detest. I recently worked on a business proposal for a musician friend that I play in several bands with. He has a desire to open a music store and actually owned a music store in partnership with his father when he was much younger. We were so excited to describe all the future goals and marketing strategies for the bank to review in our proposal. He has a good job, good money, but this was his desire at age sixty, to own a music store. I projected that in five years he will have paid the bank back for the upfront capital in full and will at age sixty-five be able to also collect his Social Security check and have profit from this music store, with his loan repaid. His reputation for excellence resonates from him and shows in every area of his life. This will be a successful business should he decide to move forward.

You can remake your career even at sixty years old if you want it bad enough. There is a song by Don Henley called "How Bad Do You Want It." It's a great song. Don't let your disappointments in the past corrupt your future endeavors. This will cause you to not be ambitious and your fears will take control of your future, leaving you with more regrets. As I discovered, uncertainty can actually feel worse than the bad outcome you're afraid of.

Two studies by Sarah A Burgard, PhD, associate professor of sociology and epidemiology at the University of Michigan, found that people whose jobs are chronically insecure reported significantly higher rates of depression, and poorer health, than those who had actually lost their jobs.

Apparently uncertainty itself is so hard to bear that it makes people assume the worst. Many people tend to equate uncertainty with a negative outcome, even when the likelihood of a bad result isn't very high. Uncertainty by definition means you don't know how something will turn out, which means that a happy outcome is just as possible as an unhappy one. In one university study, respondents were actually wrong 85 percent of the time when they predicted that some unresolved issue in their life would turn out badly. Think of all that worry for absolutely nothing. Sometimes the thing we dread turns out to be just the kick in the pants we need to move in a new and even more fulfilling direction. So if you are worried about being laid off, have an honest talk with your boss about your concerns. Admittedly, sometimes there's no clear map of action, and you might have to be creative. Be bold if there is something on your bucket list you want to try. Get the information, research it, and let opportunity take hold of your ideas.

What is important most about this entire first chapter is to look at these separate areas of your life and decide to run your own race! I named the book *Run Your Own Race* for a reason. No matter what others think about your health, your career, your weight, your organization skills, your marriage or lack of, they are not you! You have more power than you may realize to live happy. Take what you can use from these twelve chapters. See how they will work for you as tools that can fit into your lifestyle. Be open to the way you think about things. To what extent you utilize them is only determined by you.

Women Are More Open to Improvement and Change

Women tend to be the readers of self-help books and are usually searching for personal improvement. Women also are typically meek. Meekness is not weakness. Meekness is controlled strength. This strength under control is just like a racehorse that has been tamed. He can run very fast and hard, but also can be stroked and be very gentle. The horse is still very strong and controlled. Women tend to want to be everything to everybody. But as we get into our later years, fifty plus, we run dry and seek books that will somehow help us to be able to give without running dry. There was a song written by the Bee Gees that had the lyrics "I just want to be your everything." Nobody can sustain being anybody's everything. After your kids are grown, you've had a job or a career, which included being out of bed at a ridiculous hour in the morning for as long as you can remember. Now the icing on the cake is you finally think you have your husband trained. You no longer desire at fifty-plus to be someone's everything, and you certainly don't want someone to be your everything.

Autonomy

The importance of autonomy to women is something I cannot express enough. Later in the chapter on marriage, it is imperative to have autonomy to manage and survive misogynistic relationships. I have always been a big believer in autonomy. Autonomy means it allows you to be interested in what you want or enjoy, without regard to a partner or anyone else enjoying it or having judgment about it. Don't limit yourself. Don't lose your autonomy in your fifties because this is what makes you who you are. There is nobody exactly like you. It would be a boring world if we all had the same personality, tastes, passions, and dreams. Utilize the Internet to search for books about a subject matter you are dealing with or striving to understand or wanting to learn about. I am a fan of girls' night gatherings, and we discuss books and subjects to better each other rather than mindless gossip. We discuss problems with knowledge and a general collaboration for how to best handle them. This is productive learning and brainstorming and gathering of friends that can help push each other to a higher level with just one idea or stretching a subject much deeper. It's also a great way to try new healthy recipes and alcoholic drinks with each other. It serves as a connection for you and your friends. Think of ten positive people and send out invitations to gather for an evening of conversation and spirits. I know this can be a stretch outside of our comfort zone if we aren't naturally social. Perhaps if you are not inundated with lots of friends, talk to your neighbors over some wine in gatherings.

Autonomy should be the single most important thing to encourage your retired husband to consider to keep busy. This would be something he enjoys regardless of whether you like it or are involved with it or not. Should anything happen to you, he will have something to fall back on. It will serve as a great outlet for a woman who is retired or facing retirement as well. Find something only you enjoy. A book club, a gym, a cooking class, a musical instrument.

There was a story about a man who was watching a fisherman out on a lake. The fish were biting, and he was catching lots of fish. He noticed that when the fisherman would catch a big fish, he would throw it back into the lake, but every time he would catch a small fish, he would keep it. This continued until he had caught five or six small fish. After a while of observing this, the man who was watching finally walked over to the fisherman and asked, "Why do you throw back the big fish and only keep the small fish?" The fisherman replied, "I only have a five-inch frying pan, and those fish were bigger than five inches and wouldn't fit."

How often do we live our lives like that? The fisherman would limit himself rather than buy a bigger frying pan! This is a perfect example of how we accommodate where we are, instead of change to accommodate where we are going. We are meek enough to read self-help books, but we need to have the controlled strength to accommodate where we are going and use the gifts within ourselves that are uniquely our own.

Autonomy must have a component that is necessary for true autonomy. You cannot consider anything that would require your spouse or significant other to be involved. Don't buy a two-man kayak for your passion to do something you enjoy because it would require another person to be involved. Buy a single-man kayak. Autonomy is what only *you* enjoy. Don't join a couple's tennis team. Join a singles team. You can't expect a spouse to necessarily enjoy what you are passionate about. Find friends who enjoy those same things even if it may not be your spouse, that's OK. There will be lots of similar activities you may enjoy that match your spouse's level of equal enjoyment. If you expect your husband to pretend to enjoy something, it will cause underlying pressure, and it will eventually cause an eruption later. Guaranteed, probably when you least expect it! Run your own race!

This very thing occurred when I was very active in the band and was doing shows every weekend. This was not work to me as I enjoyed packing the drums and reassembling them at the venues and playing for four hours and then tearing down and repacking them back into the trailer. But my husband was helping me do it just to be nice and really wasn't enjoying it. It should have been a passion that only I enjoyed. When someone doesn't enjoy something, they become impatient and begin drudging through it like it is a chore. I am very independent, and I could hook up my own trailer and load my equipment. For the last few years I had the help of my personal "roady" (drum tech), Helen, who is a special longtime friend. It became very apparent, while loading and unloading equipment, that there was underlying resentment from my husband by his demeanor, and soon I made a decision to release my husband from any expectations toward helping with my band. This was *my* autonomy and passion. Now he waits up for me at home, makes me coffee before I leave for the show, and helps me hook up the trailer to my SSR convertible car. That is all the support that is needed from him with no strings or animosity attached on my part. He can have time to enjoy a whole night in front of the TV, while I am playing my drums out at a nightclub or private event. It's a win for both of us.

Everybody needs to respect autonomy and have something that only they personally enjoy. Later in life you will be glad you explored something you enjoyed. It is easy to do things together, but when you are alone due to divorce, death, or retired with your spouse, autonomy will be your saving grace.

My husband came face to face with his lack of autonomy when we were separated for a year. He took up the hobby of racing a small RC toy race truck. He began going to the track weekly. It was something he enjoyed for himself. He met a few retired guys there, and it gave him a social outlet. Men typically have fewer friends than women, so men need to learn the value of autonomy for later as well. Encourage your spouse to explore a new hobby or a fun hobby that may have been tabled for a few years due to raising children or lack of income. Revisit something you or your spouse may have wanted to get involved in for fun together additionally.

Organization

When I was teaching aerobic dance every morning and every evening in the 1980s and '90s, I began reading a book called *Turning Clutter and Chaos to Order*. It was a book that used a card file system where you must use 3×5 cards with tasks written out and put in a card file box. This was long before computers and laptops were the normal, or cell phones for that matter. I used this card file system of structuring the tasks in my life into daily, weekly, monthly tasks, and color-coordinated cards would indicate if it was a daily job, weekly job, monthly, or annual task. I became very proficient using the system in my own life and home. I decided to create a class based on this book, and using the card file system, I created an outline for a class and course curriculum. I took it down to Clover Park Technical College and met with the president of the college. I showed him the course outline I had created, and he was very happy to place me on the schedule for instructing an evening class. I taught the class at the college one day a week as a six-week course. I was thrilled to be able to teach this class and help other women channel their efforts in a more effective organized fashion, making their lives easier. I taught this class for several years at Clover Park Vocational Technical College and soon had satellite classes at other schools. I created visual aids for clarity. I laugh when I recall getting a phone call from a student who was attending the class. She was distraught and crying and needed to be encouraged. I was in the middle of painting a cabinet in the kitchen on a ladder, straddling the phone on my shoulder, paintbrush in my hand and my three-year-old son Nicholas was playing with toys on the kitchen floor. I was able to give her the support she needed and ease her frustration. Organization makes your life less stressful. It is tough to do the initial organizing, especially if it doesn't come naturally, even harder to keep everything in its place after that. But it is worth the effort. I would highly recommend this book *Turning Clutter and Chaos to Order*. Even being an outdated book, the principles are great. It is easy to learn how to take control of your life just simply by organization. Organization allows time for yourself, but still accomplishing your goals for keeping up with your home, your responsibilities; giving you more free time as a result.

Have you ever straightened up a friend's cupboard or closet or even your own only to find that in three weeks they look like an explosion occurred? Here are some tips.

1. Own at least one file cabinet and a box of hanging files with labels.
2. File everything.
3. Make a file for warranties and booklets.
4. Put in a file box every booklet for each appliance you own including yard tools, stereo equipment, etc., that comes with a booklet or manual. Each

new thing you buy with a booklet in the future goes into this file. No exceptions. Attach receipt to the booklet too.

5. Make a file for bank statements, and any papers or bills you get on a monthly basis. Label them specifically. File them each month. This only takes a minute and makes it easy to research anything later, plus alleviates any papers lying around in a pile. Use a small basket to put current bills into as they come in each month.

6. Make a file for Christmas gift ideas. Jot it down and stick it in the file with the name of the person whom you were thinking for the gift.

7. Make a file for everything. Include tax deduction receipts for the current year, health insurance, and car insurance. Literally everything must have a file if it is a paper you will later possibly need to refer to in the future.

8. Give everything a home. Nail polishes go in a basket or a box. Paper clips go in a desk drawer in a designated container. Reading glasses are in each room for convenience as is scissors and pens, rubber bands, etc., in specific drawers.

9. Put things back. It doesn't do you any good if you get organized and then don't discipline yourself to take the 2.2 seconds to put it in the drawer, hang it up, throw it away, or wash it off. Slow down and live in the moment. There is no emergency to prevent you the time to keep organized and stay organized. Tell yourself to

put it away where it goes. When you are retired, you will have lots of time, so what's the hurry? Put things back where they belong. You'll have all day!

10. Go through and streamline your home. This means start at your front door and move clockwise along the wall into each bedroom, bathroom, and closet and storage space utilizing the boxes described below.

It's all about the purses and accessories, some women will say! Bend old-fashioned wire hangers' shoulder ends up on both sides. This will leave the wire to hold handles for the purses. Purse hangers make it easier to choose colors and styles. Also use creative holders for belts and bracelets such as wooden racks for drying dish plates, which can be turned sideways and mounted to the wall for hanging belts. Use your imagination!

To streamline your home, you need the following:

- Goodwill giveaway box
- Keep box
- Sell
- Throwaway box

Your motto while streamlining should be:

If you haven't used it, worn it, played with it, or remembered you even owned it in twelve months, say good-bye! Streamline your entire house that way.

Letting go is difficult if you are sentimental in nature. Seasonal items are obviously a case by case, but if the kids' outdated ski equipment is still hanging in the garage and they are now married and moved out, it's time to organize and streamline your life. Christmas decorations can begin to look pretty tattered and worn out as we age, so consider starting fresh with new items.

Give yourself several months to complete this streamlining, spending extra time in your kitchen. Keep your kitchen tendencies in mind when repositioning your different cooking and baking bowls, glasses, plates, and pantry items. Take everything out of every cupboard and wipe as you go. New places for kitchen gadgets can make a big difference for working with your spouse in a small space preparing meals. Keeping that in mind, think what makes sense for your preparation tendencies for convenience such as coffee items close to coffee pot, etc. Allow yourself only one *junk drawer* in your home. I suggest a medium-size basket by your stairs if you have a two story and use this basket to collect shoes, earrings, and anything that needs to go upstairs to its proper place and put away. When you make fewer trips up the stairs, you save time and energy put to better use. Never walk upstairs without taking something that needs to go upstairs eventually anyway. Work smarter, not harder.

Don't allow consumerism to overtake your life in the future. Always ask yourself the question before you purchase anything from now on, Do I *want* this or Do I *need* this?

Use Your Strengths and Weaknesses

If you enjoy a particular household task and don't mind the time you invest in doing the task, communicate this to your spouse. Utilize each other's enjoyment of everyday chores or tasks. For instance, I enjoy washing dishes. It is my Zen time where I can get warmed up by the hot, soapy water. I can look out my window and see a tree greenbelt of evergreen trees. I also watch robins in the cement birdbath positioned outside to view from the kitchen window. While I'm doing the dishes, I rarely expressed how much I like to wash dishes to David. David always assumed that I detested this job because *he* doesn't enjoy doing dishes. The dishwasher is faster and easier, but when I do them by hand, it is my quiet time, and I enjoy the outcome and reward of a clean kitchen. To be truthful, however, on more than one occasion when I have been in a hurry, I had huffed and slammed my way through the ordeal of loading or unloading the dishwasher. I have even broken a few dishes by accident just because I was in a hurry at that moment. Time constraints make us rush through a job we may normally enjoy doing. An obligation or a deadline makes us resent having to do it. Worse than that, resentment can build even more intensely when we allow ourselves to think *"clearly he has time to do it."* But beware of unrealistic expectations of each other. He may not care about the things you care about. You probably don't care about the things he finds a priority either.

Pick the tasks that you love to do. Use each other's strengths as assets. Several of my friends love to do the laundry. The folding or laying out of clothing items is Zen time. Personally, folding socks while I watch TV or a movie or talk on the phone is enjoyable to me. Your spouse may like to do laundry or enjoys cooking and derives pleasure doing it. Now with retirement in play, you can discuss this and allow his tasks to comingle with your tasks and use this pattern to apply toward all your strengths and weaknesses. Make a list of your most favorite and least favorite daily tasks.

Making the list is the hard part. Don't procrastinate about discussing which chores are enjoyed and which are detested. Start with his weaknesses, as we can point the finger much more easily. He may hate doing the finances and paying bills, and it is always a frustration to him. *If he doesn't enjoy it, he won't be good at it!* A red flag that this is probably not his strength is when overdrafts come up continually by accident. Capitalize on his strengths. Allow each other to utilize the things you are good at. You may be excellent at keeping track of things and filing things. Perhaps you should start doing the bills and bookkeeping for a month or two. He can show you what may be significant and important to begin taking over the task. It's a team effort to be retired together.

The hardest part to keep in mind and avoid is animosity! Don't feel like you are being upstaged. He may be doing it better than you were able to do it. You are a team, so he is your *best* team mate. It is his strength if he does it well. You could give him a task that you detest or do not enjoy, and he will excel at it! Taking his strength and giving him the opportunity to handle that task merely helps make a happy household. You can have no animosity even if he relieves you of a task and blatantly outshines or amazes you. Say nothing! It's a wonderful thing because it's using his strengths to compensate for your weaknesses to create a happy environment.

Write down each task and write down each strength and weakness or tendency. If you really know each other well it should take ten minutes to make a list and cross match which person can best tackle the task. This includes tasks such as vacation planning, dish duty, laundry duty, bill paying, vacuuming, watering plants, cutting grass, washing cars, chemical maintenance in Jacuzzi tub, and many more tasks you can think of. There is no house fairy that magically takes care of everything.

Women Use Food to Cope

This is much more common now than even a decade ago. It is very evident as you observe the average woman who is in her fifties. Food, alcohol, drugs, even sex, are all coping mechanisms, but the easiest and quickest to attain to fill the dopamine fix is food. Keep a diary or chart of what you eat and when you eat! This will help you acknowledge the stresses that cause you to eat.

Working in my real estate office, I remember I would have espresso beans that were chocolate covered on my desk at work. When I was doing a high volume of transactions, I found that I would be on the phone having an intense conversation standing and leaning against my desk. I would pop an espresso bean in my mouth, and then when I would be discussing something stressful, I would continue to pop them in my mouth, one right after another, call after call, until my hands were shaking and I was talking really fast. It took the edge off at the time, but having them readily available on my desk was lethal to my diet as well as my ability to control myself and cope with stress correctly. I changed my pattern and removed the espresso beans from my desk and soon didn't miss them. It can be an oral thing as well to deal with stress. Chewing gum worked for a replacement—sugar-free, of course.

Chewing gum is helpful and actually curbs your appetite and satisfies you, making your brain feel satisfied. Your brain won't tell you that you are hungry when chewing gum even when you are grocery shopping and its dinnertime. Try it. You will amaze yourself. This is partly why smoking is difficult to overcome aside from the nicotine. The oral stimulation is soothing and used in coping. For me gum is helpful.

Biting your nails during an intense movie or stressful moment is a coping mechanism similar to using food to cope. Once we recognize the triggers that cause us to eat or smoke or bite our nails, then we can manage this behavior and change to a different behavior. Pay attention to yourself and even chart this behavior by writing down in your journal circumstances surrounding your temptations with food or stress triggers.

I keep a fingernail file by my chair while watching TV to give myself something to do rather than bite my nails. As a child I struggled with nail biting. I file them or polish them. Try shelled sunflower seeds while watching TV. This makes it more difficult to eat quickly and gives the oral sensation for your brain. I collect and paste recipes on blank scrap paper and put in three ring binders for future meals or parties. I do this while watching TV. Any hobby you can do in front of the TV will eliminate eating. Keeping busy with your hands is an important key element to not eating at night.

I keep a word find book that you can pick up at the dollar store to find words while on the phone and placed on hold instead of grabbing a bag of chips to munch on. While chatting on the phone, I keep busy organizing a drawer or cabinet, doing dishes by hand or folding laundry rather than eat. How easy it is to demolish a bag of Lay's potato chips mindlessly one at a time while chatting with a friend. I even have a competition with myself to see if I can empty the dishwasher in less than two minutes, setting the timer on the microwave. It is a workout just putting things in their proper place quickly but orderly. My spoons and forks are placed neatly back to back and not just tossed in the silverware drawer. I keep trying to beat the clock. You can come up with productive games like this to do while on the phone rather than eating and having guilty regrets later.

Watch out for those peanut butter sandwiches that you make for the grandkids especially if you are a regular babysitter. Even licking the knife every day is a habit, and it adds calories and the extra we don't need. Controlled strength means to say no and rinse off the peanut butter from the knife before placing it in the dishwasher. Go ahead and let it go to waste. The few cents in cost is not worth compromising your goal of being disciplined. Ziploc bags and containers were made for leftovers if you can't throw food away. I must admit, what was most helpful for me to cope with food was being busy. Spending time practicing new music material on my drums in the evenings kept me from evening snacking. For me the general rule was no eating after 8:00 p.m. Studies show your body needs *downtime* during sleep and should not be digesting food from a late-night snack. For you, this evening pattern change could be time for a sewing project, such as a Christmas gift for a grandchild, painting a room or reading a book in the bathtub, even go to bed early. Finding something constructive to exchange for eating should be a serious consideration. Focus on a craft, project, or anything to help cope with our fast-paced lifestyle. Demands we put on ourselves and the additional pressures and expectations others put on us can be a contributing factor to our desire to soothe ourselves with food. This exchange of doing something constructive instead of eating when you are the most vulnerable can make a big difference. This can allow you to turn your focus on another enjoyable dopamine fix that uses the same brain receptors as an ice cream cone produces. To control how you cope with stress and not use food to cope has to be the most difficult of all coping mechanisms. Commercials on TV glorify food in bright colors and happy people. Psychologically it is conditioning our thinking to equate happy people with consuming food. You never see a commercial on TV with someone eating ice cream with a sad frown on their face.

Sugar is extremely addictive. Limit your sugar intake, not by using Splenda or artificial sugar, but by eating fruit instead. Understand that sugar is physically addictive and is driven by your brain and you have no control over it. It would be difficult to have a cookie jar of cookies sitting on the counter staring at you every day subconsciously tormenting you. Finally, after resisting you give in to it and indulge. Don't sabotage yourself by buying what you think your partner or grandkids would want. They are most likely addicted to sugar too! Offer them the same healthy choices of fruits and low-sugar alternatives as you are eating. Once you become less accustomed to sugar in your system, your brain will not crave it. That's how the brain works. But you must go cold turkey. Just like an alcoholic or drug addict cannot use a little alcohol or a little of their drug of choice while getting clean and creating new habits. A no-sugar policy will work for as long as you can tolerate it, and when it's been several weeks, you can add small, reasonable amounts only on occasion. Choose from the list in the earlier chapter of "Super Foods That Power You Up." You can enjoy food to the fullest but keep the motto *"You eat to live, not live to eat."* If you are constantly obsessing on your meals, thinking about food, or worrying when you will be eating next, doesn't that sound like an addict? It should not control you or your dominant thoughts or be used to cover up your sadness or stress. People who suffer from addictive personality disorders are often battling the bulge and struggle to maintain their weight.

Here are suggestions to help cope with eating:

1. Keep busy.

2. Chew gum (especially when you're hungry).

3. Find projects you enjoy and start new ones on a continuous basis.

4. Work on projects during your vulnerable eating tendencies.

5. Ignore commercials on the television (they never look as good in real life when you order them).

6. Do an activity during phone calls to keep your hands busy.

7. Remind yourself, you *"eat to live, not live to eat"*.

8. Read the labels for sugar content in everything (power bars, frozen items, canned goods)

9. Diligently make an effort to avoid sugar for several weeks and afterward limited occasions only.

Counseling services may be an option to seek out help to find the triggers that can cause the emotional eating you may be struggling with.

Massage therapy is also a helpful alternative to cope with the stress we endure as we age. We are the "sandwich generation" because we are taking care of our children or grandchildren at the same time as taking care of our parents, as we are living much longer due to improved medical miracles and better health care coverage.

Women Use Alcohol or Pot to Cope

This is such a controversial subject but must be addressed especially since pot has recently been legalized in some states. It can be used in the comfort of your own home and treated with the same respect and responsibility as alcohol regarding driving and appropriate times to use it.

Many of us experimented in the '60s, '70s and '80s with pot (marijuana), and some enjoyed it more than others. I personally put my best choreography for dance classes together while under the influence of pot in my dance days in the '80s. It got me through to the end of some long days at my nail salon business in the '90s while filing fingernails all day after listening to women explain their complicated problems and difficulties. Back then it was not as strong or pure as we can get today. It has finally lost its stigma, however, for being categorized as the same status and addictive components as crack or heroin or methamphetamine.

It is a weed that has been around a long, long time. There are many who will never be comfortable using marijuana regardless of whether it is legal or not. But many believe that this plant that grows naturally in the ground as a "weed" requiring little care has been put on earth by God for our consumption. Never changing its structure during its growth or altering it with any chemicals or extra ingredients, just simply letting the daylight change with the season. It buds out naturally for consumption as the days get shorter. As a cigar would be consumed in a man's easy chair at the end of a long day, or a glass of wine at the end of a long week, marijuana is commonly consumed with the same purpose for a relaxation effect.

I have been counseling many women and couples where marijuana is consumed as a balancing aid. I use a test as a guide to consumption of marijuana or anything from coffee to energy drinks to alcohol and food. The test is to ask yourself, Does this enhance my life in a positive way, giving me the relaxation I need without any negative effect to others around me? Obviously falling down drunk around family or friends would be an easy answer for consuming alcohol. But it is not easy if you are not paying attention to measuring the balance it *has* in your life. Some clients I counsel who have had past drug use such as methamphetamine or heroin don't like how marijuana makes them feel, so they must find another avenue for relaxation. Using marijuana or alcohol as a coping mechanism is different from using it as a balance for help with relaxation. Coffee and energy drinks are consumed to help with an extra lift you may need for a task or project. Use of marijuana, kept in balance, not negatively affecting others, allows you permission to run your *own* race as you want without regard to how others may judge you. I suspect there will be lots of pot smokers in heaven who love the Lord and have a close relationship with God, to many folks' astonishment! Be careful if you are consuming pot or alcohol on a regular basis, however, because it can have an effect on you, more than you realize. Just like food, it should not be a coping mechanism. Great to enjoy if it gives you the effect you want, makes you happy, helps you with conditions such as carpal tunnel, headaches, or allows you to calm your mind and focus on what is important. But everyone is different.

Other ailments documented such as epilepsy in young children who have hundreds of seizures a day. After being given THC in oral oil doses, they can go days without seizures. "A miracle cure," many mothers have said. One mother began crying while watching their three-year-old splashing in the water for the first time instead of lying in bed in a vegetative state being told that the brain needs to rest, threatening to induce a coma for that purpose. Using an oil-based product extracted from THC has proven to bring joy to many parents with epileptic children.

Recently a veteran told how he could not stop the panicked dreams and nightmares. He was now a retired seventy-one-year old helicopter pilot who was diagnosed with post-traumatic stress disorder. He said he took sleeping pills for years after he retired. Then he found a more satisfying alternative: just a few hits off a pipe or bong and he doesn't have the dreams anymore. Faced with a skyrocketing suicide rate, this could conceivably change our approach to medicine. Cannabis therapy could help many veterans reduce their dependency on opiates. Government statistics showed twenty-two veterans commit suicide each day.

One very interesting factor to consider for women and the use of marijuana: our ability to utilize both sides of the brain at the same time, which is great for allowing us to think of multiple things at once. However, many women I have spoken to have found that their mind begins working so fast in so many directions at the same time. Using marijuana will help settle them and help them focus. It slows down their brains, in a sense, and diminishes anxiety. If you think of a mouse running on an exercise wheel going around and around in a circle with no end in sight, that is how many women feel on a daily basis. Marijuana calms this intense circle for a short time. Many women who may unknowingly suffer from ADD or ADHD or an anxiety disorder may find relief with marijuana. The alternative is antidepressants. Most women I speak to about antidepressants report that the adverse side effects are awful.

Regardless, marijuana shouldn't interfere with your life and should merely *balance* your life. Some people say it makes them more creative and active. Lots of people say it makes them want to clean everything in sight. In some it may produce an eagerness to eat, still others to sleep or veg out on the couch all day.

Running your *own* race and pursuing happiness means you determine if the use of marijuana enhances your level of happiness or not. If you tend to gain ten pounds from using it every day for a month because you eat everything in sight, that may be a reason to rethink the *balance* of the use of marijuana. Many say it opens their mind and removes some of the innermost and deepest thoughts or helps them sleep through the night, just as a beer or a glass of wine will do for some. It can give you the freedom to remember the good old days that help you feel good about your past, making you happy. Memories are sometimes locked away so deep that it takes marijuana to allow them to show up and relax and laugh again. Pay attention to how important it is in your life and be aware if it takes precedence in your life, making you neglect responsibilities, or losing your drive or ambition. This would be out of balance with your other focuses and desires. Balance is such a key to happiness.

Women Need Structure to Relax

We are creatures of habit. This is a fact. If you have ever attended classes or seminars for your work that required you to sit in a classroom for several days in a row, think about how many times you would tend to sit in the exact same seat if it was available each day you attended. I would teach real estate classes about marketing or other subjects, and I noticed that this would occur. This would help me learn their names more quickly when they sat in the same seat repeatedly, but I observed this was almost always the case. We tend to turn right more often than left. These are natural things we do, and so we can use these tendencies to our benefit.

Make a Set of Rules You Can Live With

So here are a few rules for areas of my life that I have used to structure my life. These are easy to adapt, and I believe they will create a longer and happier life. You can add to these or not utilize them at all because it is for your happiness that you would adopt these changes to run your own race.

This will help structure your life even when no one is watching. For me, I have a thing about walking past garbage on the ground. If I am doing something outside my home or getting something out of my band trailer, which I parked in the alley behind my townhome, and I see a fast-food cup on the ground, bottle, or napkin or even a gum wrapper, I will bend over and pick it up. It is just my thing. It is my rule. It only takes a second to pick up, and if nobody did this, you can imagine what our area and streets would look like. We have yard service every week at my townhome, and chances are, they will use the yard blower to remove it, but I can't stand to look at trash in the meantime, and it only takes one second to pick it up and carry it to the trashcan.

- *Have breakfast every day.* Eating a nutrient-dense breakfast including protein, whole grains, and fruit will help keep your insulin level steady all morning and prevent you from overeating later on. The National Weight Control Registry studied four thousand dieters who had lost weight and kept it off for more than six years. They found that those who ate breakfast upon rising within the first hour lost more weight. Some good choices: an egg sandwich with strawberries, or whole-grain cereal with low-fat milk and half a banana or grapefruit. Yogurt is always a great breakfast food with fruit and grape nuts sprinkled on top. My grandmother who lived until ninety-nine years old and took no medication for blood pressure, diabetes, or any other ailment always had toast and sliced strawberries on it. To this day, it is one of my favorites with coffee in the morning. Cinnamon with Kenyon pepper is also a favorite and for variety honey and cinnamon combination.

- *Drink more water.* Personally I am not a fan of plain water. When I was teaching my dance aerobic classes, I would go through many water bottles. I would always drink water at dinner. Now that I don't teach aerobic dance, I don't drink enough water. Unfortunately I prefer the dreaded sinful diet soda or coffee during the day. But I try to drink more water every day and limit my diet soda. When I drink more water for two weeks, I notice the pounds melt away. Diet drinks will disrupt our ability to properly estimate the number of calories we're consuming, so we eat more than we should. I am a lover of diet soda and try to limit it to one a day. Iced tea in the summer at least gets some water into us! Make yourself sun tea in jars outside on those nice sunny days. I grow mint in an outside planter box and muddle mint in my iced tea. Everyone laughs when they talk about someone ordering at McDonald's a Big Mac, large fries, and a diet coke! Which brings me to the next rule I have structured in my life.

- *Don't eat out for two weeks.* Dining away from home can be convenient, but you have no control over the way the food is cooked or the portion sizes. Experts estimate that restaurant portions can be three times the normal serving size. Rule of thumb: Fruits and vegetables should be the size of your *fist*, meat should be no bigger than a *deck of cards*, and fish should be the *size of a checkbook*. Avoiding eating out for just two week will give you the ability to learn good choices and portion sizes to follow you the rest of your life. Then my rule is eat out as a treat. If you are tempted to just drive through a fast-food restaurant while running errands, try a power bar with low sugar content and high protein content, this will get you through a busy day. Stash almonds and power bars in your car glove box or briefcase. Stay out of the drive-thru fast-food line! Coffee (plain, not a latte) also helps get you through that extra hour of running errands, avoiding temptation. Starbucks Coffee is banking on you needing a low-calorie cup of coffee, so enjoy one, but not the pastries. *Just say no!*

- *Inspect food labels.* Women who regularly read food labels are, on average, nine pounds lighter than those who don't practice this, research from the US National Health interview study found. You don't need a calculator. Just scan labels for calories and other nutrients. If one brand of yogurt has twelve grams of sugar and another has twenty grams, you know which to choose. I typically get probiotic plain yogurt or Greek plain yogurt and add a teaspoon of canned blueberry pie filling or fresh fruit like blueberries, kiwi fruit, and it still has a lot less sugar content and total calories than premade flavored yogurts available. Blueberries tend to turn quickly if fresh, so before they turn too ripe, use leftover blueberries in chocolate chip cookies and use half the sugar and brown sugar for scrumptious healthy cookies loaded with antioxidants.

- *Drain your meat.* I do not just drain my meats. I fry or cook the meat; then I put the meat in a doubled paper towel on a cookie sheet or bowl and squish the heck out of it, till the paper towel is saturated, and then transfer into a clean bowl or fry pan to complete my meal. Now all that fat is not in your arteries! Just my rule.

- *Snack often.* The key is smart snacking. Data studies show that people who snack twice a day lose more weight than those who eat three large meals. One snack should be between breakfast and lunch and the other between lunch and dinner. No eating after 8:00 p.m. if possible. Snacking helps keep insulin levels fairly constant, which can prevent hunger and overeating at lunch and dinner. Great healthy snacks with protein to eliminate hunger include a handful of almonds or walnuts. Baby carrots and a few pretzels or cucumbers drenched in vinegar, or a piece of fruit. Celery with peanut butter or cream cheese and crackers. Stay away from granola bars and high-sugar bars. Energy bars have various levels of sugar, so pick the lowest one. Sugar is your enemy, not necessarily fat. On your day off work, rinse carrots off and celery, cucumber slices, or any vegetable you enjoy and put in a fancy bowl and leave it on the counter with walnuts, pretzels, etc. This will allow you to munch without guilt during the day while you are home.

- *Chew gum.* Yes, chewing gum can help keep the weight off. And for reasons you may not have realized, chewing gum releases hormones that signal your brain you're full. This also helps if you are a nibbler (someone who tends to sample food while cooking or watching TV). If I am having a girls' gathering and preparing appetizers, I will chew gum. When I am on my way to rehearsal for one of my bands and I haven't had much to eat, I will chew gum then eat after band practice something light but healthy like a salad if it is after 8:00 p.m.

- *Beware of diet foods.* I can't tell you how many people I know who have gained weight on foods labeled as "low-fat" or "fat-free." Often these products are loaded with sugar to make up for the taste lost when the fat is removed. Since many diet foods are also highly processed, you end up getting fewer nutrients and lots of calories and salt. Better to eat a small helping of higher-fat food periodically. Anything by Kashi is a safe bet. Kashi makes anything from crackers to nuggets similar to grape nuts. They are known for better ingredients and less sugar and fat.

- *Get fishy.* Fish is a crucial component in our diet. It has the good omega-3 fatty acids that are needed for brain health. It is low in calories, contains important nutrients, and may lower risk of getting certain cancers. It is helpful for inflammation like rheumatoid arthritis. Fish tacos, salmon patties, tuna are easy to fix and delicious.

- *Include dairy but limit it and always use low fat.* Dairy foods are rich in calcium and vitamin D. Take a vitamin D tablet and calcium tablet daily regardless of your intake. Thirty percent of women over fifty are deficient in these two vitamins. If you eat low-fat dairy, you can lose 38 percent more weight. I prefer nondairy liquids such as almond milk or coconut milk. Fat-free half and half is a great splurge with no guilt in my coffee.

- *Embrace whole grains with moderation.* Whole grains with seeds, rye bread, brown rice, and Quinoa (pronounced Keen-wau). Limit white bread, bagels, white pasta, and all muffins.

- *Self-talk every day. "I can do this."* We talk to ourselves five hundred times a day. Allow quiet time without noise of the radio, TV, or any other influence every day for thirty minutes or more. During those quiet times, repeat to yourself only positive things like *"I can do this," "It will work out," "I know I can think of something."* Emotional flooding occurs with continuous noise. If self-talk is only negative, a person will typically flee from quiet because it will mean hearing their own negative self-talk. Earbuds for iPods and so many distractions available to avoid enduring any quiet is usually a symptom of a negative self-talker. Covering up your self-talk with noise only creates a pattern to unlearn later rather than change the self-talk to positive and not run from the quiet but embrace it.

This emotional flooding is similar to pushing the gas pedal in a car over and over and soon flooding the car, so it can't do anything. It is in a state of flooding and unable to function and won't work properly. It is completely incapacitated. Continuous noise incapacitates the brain, and it cannot rest. The fact is, you can't hear your deep down thoughts and listen to your gut while thinking about a problem or situation if you are incapacitated with noise to compete with. God is constantly giving us signals in many different ways and situations, but only if it is quiet enough to hear them.

- *Your brain is a computer you command. Take control!* "I can do this" is imputing into your brain a command, like a computer command, expecting the result to be achieved.

  Example:

  A highly skilled competitive figure skater whom I admire named Ross Miner can be seen each time before he enters the skating rink for a competition saying to his coach, "I can do this." He always puts on an almost flawless performance. Yes, maybe it would be flawless without saying that, but it does something to you inside when you use positive self-talk and verbalize it! Your brain accepts the command "I can do this" and follows it as muscle memory takes over in the case of an ice skater. It is such a great phrase, and I am convinced it works.

- *Smell does matter.* Your brain is altered by scent more than you realize. The brain responds positively and becomes happy to good scents. Here is a secret power! I was wearing perfume and body cream while in real estate, and it became apparent that it really made a difference in how people reacted to you. I would get comments at the grocery store, men who would ask their wives to find out what cologne I was wearing. It was insane. I would keep a hand cream of this in my drawer at the office to put on when I was signing papers with a couple or a gentleman to complete a transaction at the office. Put on some perfume and use the *power of the perfume* to help you make others happy (plus, nobody can be mean and nasty to you when you smell good!) Spray some cologne on the letter you are sending complaining about something. Lots of fragrances are so inexpensive for the value added to your life and happiness. It's just utilizing what is available to us for the best benefits while enjoying our lives.

- *Adjust and adapt to stress.* Use "healthy fix" responses instead of "false fix" responses when daily stresses or ongoing stresses infiltrate your life. Stop, think, and plan ahead. See chart.

STRESS	FALSE FIX RESPONSE	HEALTHY FIX RESPONSE
WORK DEADLINE	Stress eat, stay up late, drink too much caffeine, and get too little sleep	Get up from your desk every 30 minutes and stretch, sip green tea, chew gum, do mini-meditations, eat Healthy fix food every 3 to 4 hours.
SICK KIDS	Skip exercise, stress out over missed work responsibilities, lose temper, eat mindlessly, and don't sleep enough	Do yoga/Palates stretches or dance to Zumba DVD while kids sleep, nap when possible, delegate work to coworker (you'll repay) eat Healthy Fix foods every 3 to 4 hours.
BUSINESS TRAVEL	Eat airport and airplane food and buffet breakfasts, skip meals, spend late nights drinking, order room service at midnight, raid hotel minibar, and skip exercise.	Pack travel food (dried fruit, nuts, peanut butter on whole wheat); stock hotel fridge with yogurt and cottage cheese; set 11 PM curfew; use hotel gym before breakfast; drink sparkling water; sleep 7 to 8 hours.
FIGHT WITH SPOUSE	Bag exercise, watch *endless Law & Order* reruns, load up on ice cream, and drink extra wine.	Call a friend to unload. Take a walk, meditate, regroup and repair with spouse ASAP.
HOSPITALIZED PARENT	Eat from vending machine, skip exercise, skimp on sleep, and feel physically sick with worry.	Walk around hospital grounds, use stairs, bring healthy fix food in cooler, walk and stretch every 30 minutes. Meditate or pray. Call friends and family for support.

- *Never leave home without sunglasses.* Women are twice as likely as men to develop age-related macular degeneration (AMD), a serious condition of the eyes' retina that gradually destroys the sharp vision needed for common daily tasks like driving or reading. Bright light may be involved in the process that starts AMD, so make sure to carry your sunglasses with you at all times.

- *Do your kegels (pelvic floor exercises).* Pregnancy, childbirth, and aging can weaken your pelvic muscles, causing urinary leakage and incontinence. To enjoy your usual activities without fear of public embarrassment, make kegel exercises part of your daily routine (see healthtools.aarp.org/health/kegel-exercises). You can do these anytime, and no one can tell.

- *Give yourself alone time every day.* If you're sitting on a park bench going through your e-mail, you may technically be alone, but you're still answering to the needs of others. The alone time I'm talking about is the kind that really truly replenishes your spirit. It is recognized by only occurring when you're not answering to anyone's needs but your own. Sadly, most women don't allow themselves this time alone. Why does the idea of solitude make so many of us uneasy? Part of it is because there is still a social stigma attached to being alone. According to Eric Klinenberg, PhD, author of *Going Solo*, many people retain a junior high mind-set. He says, "They want to signal that they're attractive, successful and interesting, and they fear that being seen alone in a theater or restaurant will send the opposite message." The attitude I'm by myself so I must look like a loser. You must not confuse solitude with loneliness. Bobbi Emel, a psychotherapist in Los Altos, California, said, "I think women often feel that if they're not doing something productive at all times, they're being lazy." The fact is that time alone is critically important to your health. For starters, it lowers stress, which helps maintain a stronger immune system to better sleep, and helps sharpen your thinking. "When you take a breather, the prefrontal cortex in your brain gets a rest," says Susan Biali, MD, author of *Live a Life You Love*. "And we're learning that the prefrontal cortex is where a lot of our impulsive decisions come from." The more you detach and unplug, she says, the more likely you are to make better decisions at the end of a long day (like avoiding that second glass of wine or what-the-heck online shopping spree). Taking pleasure in your own company is healthy and empowering. I enjoy riding my bike to a nearby park and sitting under a tree on the grass and reading a book.

You may have habits or natural rituals to add to this list. Use your imagination to develop your own good habits and tendencies. Being a person of excellence means having a set of rules to live by that is so automatic you don't even think about it anymore.

My Personal Bill of Rights

1. I have a right to say no to anything when I feel I am not ready, or that is unsafe, or when it violates my personal boundary system.

2. I have a right to determine and honor the priorities for my life and to choose the people and things I want to have in my life.

3. I have a right to change, to grow, to mature, be healthy mentally, emotionally, physically, and spiritually.

4. I have a right to be angry with someone I love. I also have a right to forgive their offense.

5. I have a right to acknowledge and accept my own value system as appropriate for me without being subjected to the judgment or values of others.

Women Use Divorce to Find Happiness

Divorce is appealing when you are completely disgusted and on your very last nerve. We've all been there! He has done something again for the last time, and you decide in your head how much easier life would be without dealing with him. Everybody has had those thoughts if they are honest with themselves. Let's face it. If you have been married for a long time, you and your spouse have learned to tolerate each other's shortcomings and learned to adjust for each as you change and mature.

What is so different when you think about divorce at fifty plus is you could very easily make divorce happen because the kids are gone. You may still be working, but your cars may be paid for by now and maybe the house, so you could easily leave, change direction, and you may believe the result would be for an easier, stress-free life, at least that would be your desire.

I must be honest, following through the process of a divorce from a long-time marriage is much more difficult than you may think. It won't make "everything better." Think hard and long before making a clearly permanent decision and make sure that this is going to bring you the happiness you need and deserve.

It is not a quick fix and may require a short move-out time period just to make sure that you truly don't want to cohabitate any longer with your spouse.

This was what I chose to do and needed to do in my marriage. I needed to move away from the everyday lifestyle we had developed and remove myself from the rut I had helped create. This allowed me to be sure my decision was not merely based on years of built-up resentment that could be resolved with some time away from each other before addressing issues.

I would absolutely suggest that you consider a hiatus from your spouse before just walking away or getting a divorce instantly. Even if it means staying in a nice hotel for a weekly, monthly rate or if you are able to stay with a friend, relative, or in a vacant rental home you may own.

This time of separation allows him to grow and for you to grow and become who you are without regard to his schedule or the dynamics of a relationship on a daily basis. He will need to grocery shop for himself, change sheets, and feel the quietness in the evening without your presence. This is not what a man wants at all, so convincing your husband to agree to such a plan would be likely difficult. It could, however, give you the space and time you may need to become a balanced person with no one to distract you or expect from you, especially if patterns have been cemented due to familiarity.

I use the analogy of a massage therapist and a massage patient as an example for an unbalanced marriage. The unhappy partner in marriage is the one who is giving the massage and is tired of massaging and wants to stop or quit. The happy partner in marriage is the one who is receiving the massage, so of course the happy partner doesn't want the massage to stop and is very content and happy just the way it is going.

This time of separation really allows you to reflect:

- Who you are
- Schedule preference for your day
- Style of evening events
- The food you like to eat
- When you like to eat
- Places you like to go
- Time of day you like to go
- Who you are *now*…not twenty-five years ago

If this time away and the new lifestyle you are enjoying, while separated doesn't match up with the life you have had with your spouse and you are significantly *better* after some time of separation, then give yourself permission to "jump off the horse."

An analogy I would use quite often in my counseling practice is to either ride on the horse proudly in the center of the saddle (stay married) or jump off the horse with a sigh of relief (divorce). You can't be *hanging* sideways on the saddle straddling the reigns, holding on for dear life and almost dragging to the ground for very long. It's exhausting. You will wear yourself out.

Unresolved conflict is considered to be the most stressful. Studies show it will take years off your life if it continues for a long period of time. You actually build up cortisol, and that allows you to gain weight and add fat as protection against stress to your body. If your marriage isn't working, take the test of time away for a determined agreed upon amount of time and then a leap of *faith* instead of living by *fear*. The fear of being alone, having less assets, financial support, or any other scenario you feel is relevant. When it comes to relationships, you may be alone a long time. But like a bad relationship, once you have had food poisoning at a buffet, you don't exactly run out to a buffet to eat right away. Nothing good can come into your life if you don't get rid of the bad. Bad spreads quickly and sometimes quietly. If you have ever had a basket of fruit with one bad piece of fruit sitting next to the other fruit, you see it soon begins to contaminate the rest of the good fruit, making it all bad.

The Man You May Be Married To

The man you may be married to may have a lack of sensitivity to the pain he is causing you. People with character disorders have little capacity for guilt, remorse, or anxiety. These emotions are uncomfortable but very necessary monitors of our ethical and moral interactions with other people. I know there are two major types of recognized character disorders. The first is narcissists. These are people who are self-obsessed. They tend to make relationships primarily in order to be reassured of their own specialness in the world. At the other end of the character disorder spectrum were more extreme disorders called sociopaths. These are people who create a whirlwind of chaos in their lives. They use and exploit anyone who come into their lives. Lies and deception are second nature to them.

But the type of person who is not always defined and often genuinely responsible and competent in his dealings with society is the misogynist. His behavior was more focused almost exclusively on his partner. He uses for weapons *his words* and *his moods*. He may not physically abuse the woman in his life, but he systematically will wear her down through psychological battering.

Women unknowingly fall into self-denying, submissive behavior with men. Women learn these behaviors early and are consistently rewarded and praised for them. The paradox here is that the behaviors that make a woman vulnerable to mistreatment are the very ones she has been taught are feminine and lovable. This man is not a clear-cut sociopath, narcissist, or sadist. This person is defined as a misogynist, according to Dr. Susan Forward, author of *Men Who Hate Women & the Women Who Love Them*. Their choice of weapon is different than the others. They are capable of long-term relationships with one woman, and his love can be particularly hot and intense. But sadly they do everything to destroy the woman they professed to love so deeply by their behavior. A misogynist (woman hater) blames a woman for everything, wants to control how she lives and behaves. They want her to give up important activities or people in order to keep him happy. They devalue her opinions and feelings and accomplishments. They will yell, threaten, or withdraw into angry silence when you displease them. A woman will be forced to "walk on eggs" rehearsing what she will say and be very bewildered by how he can change from charm to rage without warning. He can be extremely jealous and possessive and will blame her for everything that goes wrong in the relationship.

If these patterns are what you are experiencing on a daily basis, you are involved with a misogynist. The good news is you can breathe a sigh because these character patterns can change, but you have to *do* things differently not just *think* about it differently. To help you accomplish this, I have described how these relationships work and why they work in chapter 8. There are effective behavioral techniques that can bring about important changes in your relationship with your partner and with yourself. These techniques will help you become more self-protective, more confident, more effective, and less vulnerable to the manipulation. Misogynistic partnerships are difficult to maintain without specific changes in patterns being practiced.

I use an analogy for how easily we can be pulled down and how difficult it can be to pull someone up. If a positive good person is standing on a solid chair and tries to pull the negative, unhappy person upward onto the chair, both being equal in stature and weight, gravity will make it impossible or very difficult to pull the negative, unhappy person up on the chair. But yet one easy tug on the arm from the negative, unhappy person standing below the chair, and the positive good person is pulled down immediately with little effort.

Being divorced will not give you instant happiness. This is *one person* in your life. The future happiness will be dependent upon your ability to pay attention to what makes you happy and avoiding anybody who makes you become different than you are. Do you like who you are when you are with this person? Having material stuff can be a good thing. But I must admit I spent countless nights, instead of sleeping, trying to figure out how to fit my kayaks into my Chevrolet SSR, trying to figure out how to transport or use my band trailer to transport the kayaks. How can I store them from the ceiling of my already-crowded one-car garage? I had to realize that my level of happiness was not dependent on possessing the kayaks. But it is amazing how hard it is to let things go. I believe if you let material things go, suddenly you are blessed with even more. Happiness is not based on the assets you acquire or hang on to in a marriage, nor is it guaranteed by eliminating one negative person out of your life. Happiness is based on future decisions *you* make and accepting the decisions you already have made. We have all heard the statement "When one door closes, another door opens." Financial situations change all the time with job loss so prevalent now. Having less money as a consequence from a divorce or from an unexpected company closure is the same relative outcome. It's called life. Make a plan for your happiness based on what you have to work with. Take the high road. There is less traffic up there! The story of the little frog earlier in this book describes the unknown that may be so much better than you ever imagined. You just don't know about it yet.

You Pay Attention to
What You Care About

The concept of the power to control what you are willing to pay attention to is important if you are contemplating a divorce. I have already established in the previous chapters how powerful our brains are and how we consciously pay attention to whatever we tell ourselves to be attentive to. In the same way we can subconsciously tune out what we don't want to pay attention to. It's observed through body language! It takes discipline to tell ourselves (our brains) what to take notice of and listen to. An example of this would be if we are sitting and reading the paper and we smell smoke, we would immediately divert our attention from the paper to the smoke we smell, right? If you were sitting reading the paper and the TV was on quietly in the background and the score for your favorite basketball team was being announced, you would look up and likely listen intently to it, possibly turn up the volume. It takes little discipline to pay attention to what you are interested in or what you think needs your undivided attention. The power to control your brain and alert it to pay attention to something you have no *interest in* and are *detached* from is more difficult. An example would be if a husband were reading the paper and the wife casually mentioned she would be putting a roast in the oven for dinner that night. The husband may not tell himself to pay attention. He may not even look up over his reading glasses or acknowledge that she has spoken. Later in the day it would become very apparent he tuned out her comment as her husband walks into the house with a pizza he had picked up for dinner. The husband may swear his wife never said she would be preparing a roast and truly, deep down believes that fact. Because the husband did not *divert his attention* while reading the paper, he did not listen when his wife spoke. Just because it is not useful information that the husband needed at the time (while reading the paper) does not diminish its importance. You naturally pay attention to what is important to you. It takes self-discipline to tell yourself to pay attention to something even if it is boring. Our busy lifestyle demands so much of our attention now, but we must tell ourselves when our spouse is speaking that it is a priority and discipline our thoughts and attention to listening. Without this discipline being practiced on an everyday basis while you are retired together, your efforts to communicate will become pointless. You'll soon find yourselves sitting farther away from each other, touching each other less often, and finding other friends or family members to tell your stories and events to. A woman will begin to think *"he doesn't care about this anyway, so why bother wasting my breath."* Set the example of really listening to your spouse. Be willing to discipline yourself to hear their story even if it is not really interesting and truthfully monotonous about the same topics. If your spouse matters to you, then they deserve the respect of your undivided attention. This takes practice to make a habit of diverting your attention from what you are doing. Men may have a more difficult time with this if they are married to a very talkative wife. She may mutter under her breath and not clarify when he should be listening. The wife may be involved in somebody's life that is always in a crisis mode. Ladies, you don't have to sabotage your relationship by overwhelming them with constant chatter. Find a girlfriend to meet with once a week to talk. The old saying "Less is more" would be a good thing to remember. If you have neglected finding outside friends and kept to yourself, then it's time to branch out and be more open to new acquaintances. They could end up to be a best friend. Retirement allows us more time for nurturing new friendships and spending time with each other, widening our circle, but never forgetting to take time for ourselves. Watch and see if you pay attention when your spouse speaks to you. Do you really listen?

Oblivious to the Obvious

Do you truly *cherish* the things about the person you are now married to and retired with? Do you cherish the person you are beginning a relationship with? Who are they? Do you know their true and real character? After living apart for a year in my condo during our separation, then reuniting and living together again, I can speak from experience that you finally have time to become aware of things that you like about yourself. I was no longer oblivious to the obvious. Traits that others may adore about you, your spouse may not like, likewise your spouse's habits, tastes, quality and quantity of fun is not cherished by you or easily tolerated either. That's the aha moment. The irony of it all is neither spouse is at fault. Who they are should come easily, not forced or pretended. Not ignoring the obvious is difficult. For example, if your spouse wears flannel shirts every day, and it is the same shirt for four days, you begin to wonder if you married Ray Romano from the sitcom on TV. But here is the truth, he is being who he is, and no one should expect differently, not even the spouse. He likes a relaxed and comfortable attire. If a woman wears a generous amount of makeup every day out of habit from working, this is who she is. Blame it on overly self-conscious behavior, but regardless, this is who she is! After she retires, she may continue to wear makeup faithfully, but her spouse may not like it. He may feel it brings out her wrinkles and would prefer the no makeup or more natural look. Likes and dislikes are formed very young and become ultimately who we are. Who we become from habit is different than who we become due to DNA and personality traits. The realization of *who* we are and who our spouse is was violently interrupted with jobs, kids, more kids, grandkids, and responsibilities. But the aha moment lets you clearly see that each of you deserve to be with someone who cherishes you completely, not someone who needs you or tries to complete you. A vital key to this is you make your own happiness. Your attitude to think and say often to yourself, *"You create the world you live in and how you perceive things and accept things is up to you, don't be oblivious to the obvious."* When it comes to having to change who you are, nobody should need to or want to ever change who they really are, but rather keep company with those who are likeminded. If you don't feel cherished, you should. If it is obvious your spouse doesn't accept or cherish who you are, don't be oblivious to it. You deserve to be cherished. A man loves to be loved, but it is selfish for a woman to pretend to love them just to get along, financial stability, or convenience, yet hating every minute! The word *cherish* is defined as "treasure, value, adore, love and protect." Do these attributes seem obvious about how you generally feel toward him? Do you feel the sense of value and importance from him? This should reflect where your marriage or relationship is sitting presently. It should also help with a decision that is difficult to make for a divorce, an agreed-upon separation, or worthy of your time to pay attention and create new habits. Changing course by creating new habits when you recognize and embrace each other's idiosyncrasies takes effort. Discovering who we are as a woman during menopause can be eye-opening. We can be oblivious to who we are and ignore it and not be ourselves. We can be oblivious to who our partner really is, but it changes nothing. You must acknowledge a problem or idiosyncrasy before you can address it. Recognize and acknowledge where you are and then set the bar for your current relationship and any relationship in the future to include *cherish* as the major component for spending quality time with someone. You'll enjoy spending the rest of your life with them.

Perhaps you are oblivious to the obvious because the marriage has changed so gradually you didn't notice. I call it "*convenient partner*" versus "*marriage partner.*" A partner for convenience from a long-term marriage will have obvious symptoms. If the following are common behaviors during your day-to-day relationship, then your partner should be advised to purchase a dog for companionship immediately. If you are considered to be a convenient partner, your spouse will begrudge you spending time on the phone with others and time away from them doing other interest or hobbies, thus not being fully engaged and available for them. They believe your job is to keep them happy and entertain them at all times. If you are a convenient partner from a long-term marriage, your spouse will rarely speak, and if they speak, it will be to point out something wrong with someone else or something else, never complimenting any of your efforts that are making their lives easier. If you are a convenient partner, your spouse will blame you for never being around, but rarely acknowledge your presence when you are in the same room. The exception to this is a new relationship. If you are just a convenient partner, your spouse will set the standard and rules pertaining to any activities or projects to be embark upon and only allowing it to be done in the exact order will it be tolerated. Any other way would be wrong. This includes what time things should begin and how much is acceptable to spend according to their standard or opinion. This is why owning a dog sitting on the sidelines would be a much better partner. There would be no compromising necessary as a result of anyone's input or ideas other than their own. If you are a convenient partner, you may not really have a say in anything.

If you feel like you are just a convenience to your partner, it may not be your imagination. Don't be oblivious to the obvious! Yes, men are selfish, but so are women. Both men and women will use the power of familiarity to their advantage. Both partners know what buttons to push. On the other hand, sitting around all day doing nothing, spending money shopping online, having a WIFM (what's in it for me) attitude, hardly contributing to any of the responsibilities of life and having an expectation that your partner should keep you happy and do things only your way—get a dog. A marriage partner allows grace, lots of latitude, and equality as the basis for the relationship. Just like in a new relationship, you are attentive and respectful toward each other's time and opinions. You are on your best behavior in a new relationship. This is the reason many women who separate and do some casual dating find out that men *can* be nice, respectful, and agreeable. To their disappointment, however, guys are pretty much all the same after time, just different degrees of characteristics and individualities. Characteristics should be obvious if you are looking for them. Pay attention. Don't be oblivious in your current relationship. Expect what you want. It may not be too late! Set a standard for your marriage or relationship you may need to seek in the future based on who *you* really are. It is never a partner's right to make you unhappy. They can try to make you unhappy through manipulation or condescension, but do not choose to allow them to do so. If you believe you are not convenient enough for your partner and it is obvious that they want a nonverbal, non-confrontational partner with no opinion, they should get a dog! An analogy for a relationship that may not be worth redeeming is "sometimes the squeeze from an orange isn't worth the little bit of juice you get from the squeeze." Relationships are hard work, and for some, too much work! Relinquishing the position of being the boss and holding all the power can be difficult for many relationships because it requires change. Retirement has caused a shift in the power and control, so don't be oblivious to the obvious. Equality is based on each other's personality and strengths, not necessarily on who possesses the power due to money or who is the better manipulator. Acknowledge habits or patterns that have been established in the past. Decide if it is due to a characteristic and personality trait that you can embrace or simply familiarity that is manageable and correctable with new patterns and habits. Ignorance or oblivion is not bliss.

Why do Married Women Cheat?

Finally, what drives a person to become unfaithful? Past research has suggested that infidelity is one of the leading causes of divorce. Thanks to a new study published in *Contemporary Family Therapy*, we now have an inside look into why married women cheat.

Researchers Michelle Jeanfreau, Anthony Jurich, and Michael Mong conducted case studies on four women ages twenty-four to fifty-one who cheated on their spouses and whose marriages subsequently ended in divorce. Through an in-depth analysis, researchers discovered three common risk factors that contributed to the infidelity.

1. *Lack of quality time*

    According to the study, all four women expressed a desire to spend more time with their husbands but were often denied, making them feel like a second or third priority to their husbands' jobs or social lives.

    Bella, forty-eight, began her affair three years into her marriage and said she often felt anger toward her husband for leaving her constantly. "After we had our first child, he'd come in from work, take his bath. I had supper ready, (he'd take) a little nap, get up, and go out partying all the time and leave me home with the kids."

    Similarly, thirty-six-year-old Kate, who cheated on her husband after five years of marriage, said their lack of together time led to constant fighting. "He started coming in late at night, and he would leave early in the mornings and it's like we never saw each other," she explained to researchers. "We would always argue. I wanted him to spend more time with me, and he would always make other plans...do his own thing."

    The women, as the researchers explained, felt their husbands were not reciprocating the same level of desire to maintain a strong connection in the marriage, which made them susceptible to finding that connection elsewhere.

2. *Inability to resolve conflict*

An inability to communicate often leads to relationship conflicts going unresolved. In these particular cases, the lack of resolution or change in future behavior left the women feeling frustrated, and many voiced a concern that while problems were recognized, no progress was made to fix them.

"We would try and he would say, you know, I'm (going) to do better…and he never would," said Kate.

Linda, fifty-one, who divorced after twenty-one years of marriage but started cheating just six years in, said she and her ex simply failed to address the root of their conflicts. "I'd usually just leave until he cooled off, and then I'd come back and pout and say nothing to him."

The researchers concluded that a *lack of communication* was a precursor to cheating: "In each case, the attraction to marital infidelity began to grow for the women because the unresolved issues continued to be a source of conflict in the marital relationship, pushing the women further away from their spouses."

3. *Lack of attention*

Through the study, it became clear that all the women craved more intimacy in their marriages. This void was eventually filled by an affair partner.

135

Bella began thinking about an affair when "somebody started showing me the affection that I needed…the touching and feeling and being wanted."

Zoie, twenty-four, who began cheating just seven months into her marriage, said that her husband wouldn't give her even five minutes of attention, whereas her affair partner would talk to her about anything and everything.

Linda, however, summed up the women's desires best. "I want somebody in my life that would love me for me. That would just show attention to me for me…And you know made me feel like I was worthwhile. It was just somebody there to have attention with, show me attention…make me feel better about myself," she said.

What does it all mean? According to the researchers, *none of the women actively sought out affairs.* As time went on, however, they grew more frustrated in their marriages and the partner they cheated with became more desirable. When the opportunity arose, there was less hesitation to stray.

Of course, every marriage is different, but the authors of the study noted that these specific insights into cheating could help individuals and professionals identify early warning signs. After recognizing the signs in relationships, an effort can be made toward changing behavior to lessen the inevitable outcome which would be unintended.

Women Want to Look Pretty, but Don't Know How

Do we skip making ourselves a sandwich for lunch? If you time yourself on how long it takes to make yourself a sandwich, you will find it takes about ten minutes. Just ten minutes is also the time it takes to put on some makeup and look presentable. But are we willing to? You don't skip feeding yourself but often skip looking presentable. In ten minutes you can give your skin some moisture, a light coat of makeup or tinted sunscreen to even out your skin tone, some blush, mascara on your eyelashes, eye shadow accents, which are optional, lipstick and eyebrows penciled lightly. Done! This may seem like a waste of time if you are not going out anywhere and are just planning to spend the day alone doing a project, sewing or reading a book, baking a pie or anything away from the public. But you may be surprised how much it may help you psychologically feel happy and better about yourself when you take the time. The time it takes to make a sandwich you can make yourself feel pretty. It's proven that if you stay in slippers and sweats during the day, you feel sluggish. Likewise, by not putting your makeup on or doing something with your hair on your day off when you are staying at home, you feel physiologically less attractive. This alters your mood causing you to not feel good about yourself. Getting yourself presentable with the minimum basic steps also comes in handy when you decide to run to the store for something quick for your projects or get an unexpected visit from a friend. Eliminate the temptation to skip the makeup and do the unthinkable, which is going out in public looking like you just crawled out of bed. When you retire with your spouse, will this mean you will never get ready for the day since you no longer have a job? I'm sure your spouse would like you to be presentable even at home as well as when you go somewhere with them. Many times I put my minimum required makeup, sunscreen, and do my hair, only to remove it all at the end of the evening before getting ready for bed and brushing my teeth, never having left the house. It was not a waste because I felt better when I looked in the mirror all day! I looked good for others and myself.

I look completely different when I have no makeup on whatsoever. I look like a ghost, with wrinkles. If I take just ten minutes to put on my makeup, the happiness I get from it is worth the effort and discipline it takes.

Fixing yourself food should not trump fixing your looks. Your desire to fix food is your craving to eat, and you prioritize to fulfill that need. Your desire to fix your appearance should be just as important to feel good about yourself all day long. *It's never a question of time. It's a question of priority.* We all have the same twenty-four hours. It's what we do with it and what we prioritize that sets us apart and can makes our day go much better. If you will try taking the ten minutes for twenty-one days regardless of your schedule, you will find this to be true. It will eventually become a habit and second nature. The exception is days where you are sick or fighting a cold or flu and are in bed all day.

I have had many occasions where I have been working on my drums for hours at the house and someone would come to the door and I had reserved the ten minutes to make myself pretty earlier that day and said to myself "I'm so happy I took that time."

One makeup tip: When you are removing your leftover makeup around your eyes, try using moisturizing lotion like "dramatically different moisturizing" by Clinique. It is far more effective and gentle around our eyes and less drying than eye makeup remover. Just a tip!

Most of us are not considered self-conscious about our appearance to a large degree. I have always had a high level of self-consciousness, above the normal, but it has worked to my benefit. I believe my happiness is greater due to my habit or effort to look pretty and keep my standards up to what I feel is appropriate. I run my own race! Women who don't make an effort to regularly look pretty are observed to have less confidence and don't feel as happy with themselves. They don't get the same customer service at a restaurant or at a department store, and unfortunately they don't understand why. This is why! The little extra effort gives you credibility and makes you appear above average, remember the description of a person of excellence. Now that you acknowledge the problem and it only takes ten minutes to fix, why would anyone not choose to take ten minutes? Even if it is the bare minimum for staying home. I recently heard a good friend remind me of a great old saying, "If you want to stop somebody from doing something, throw a little effort in front of them!" *Anyone can do nothing!*

I treated my work appearance in the same way while owning my nail salon and real estate career. Many times I had no appointments scheduled at my real estate office, but I always dressed up with makeup as if I did have an appointment. This was when I was new to real estate and had just started at Windermere Real Estate after getting my license. I had no clients buying or selling. Many times I never had anyone come into the office, but many times I would have to show homes unexpectedly or sit down and discuss selling their home. I was ready and had the respect that came with the first impression. I felt good about myself because I looked good. Dress for success was one of the subjects I taught when I was teaching my organization course at Clover Park Vocational College as well as a class on the subject many years later for real estate clock hours required by the state of Washington. I had taught a dress for success class because I could see the changing of attire at banks and high level positions. Once respected positions become more casual, the level of trust and credibility is limited simply by the first impression. Dressing professionally has been lost due to mediocrity.

Mediocrity is so prevalent and considered normal and has become acceptable. Complacency and mediocrity is the easy way out. It does not give the character I want to be judged by because it is average. Anyone can be average! We can strive to be *above average* with very little effort. It's not like the world or society has a very high bar to reach. Just ten minutes is not a lot of time to be above average. Just a little makeup, an additional five minutes to pick out something nice to wear with complementing earrings and accessories and you are ready. That is not a lot of time to invest. Planning your outfit the night before can make this process even easier. Many times I would lay out everything for the next day, including accessories for appointments at the counseling center. I would plan out ahead of time the outfits I wear on stage at my band shows, and to prevent any mistakes, I would always completely put on what I would be performing in, all the way to my shoes. Then I put it in a garment bag to bring with me and change just before the performance. I would get pretty sweaty unloading and setting up my drums for an hour beforehand, so changing wasn't an option. It was absolutely necessary.

Unfortunately we live in a very judgmental society, and we cannot change this fact or the general perception. We can, however, adapt to the social expectation and use organization tricks to allow us to take the small amount of time to look pretty.

Organize your jewelry by color so it takes only a few minutes to pick something out, rather than pick and hunt through a whole bunch of mismatched earrings! Jewelry armoires are inexpensive and effective. Line up and match up your shoes in your closet on racks or shelves for a quick grab. Don't throw them in an unruly pile. My purses are on hangers for display with the wire shoulder part pulled up to hold several on the hangers draping over each wire

Let's be honest and admit that if the news stations had anchorwomen reporting who were plain Janes or as some folks call them "Walmart shoppers" in appearance and attire, it would not be enjoyable for most of us to watch, not to mention they would not be on the air very long. Call it shallow, superficial, or whatever you want, but our society dictates that it is appropriate to look pretty.

If you don't know how to begin a ritual of skin care and makeup, then take a day to go to a makeup counter at the local mall and ask them to do a makeup consultation to get the most out of expert advice. This will give you a basis you can begin with. You can purchase your makeup anywhere, but knowing the basics will help and inspire you. Things I do consistently when it comes to makeup may be similar to what habits you currently following.

1. Put a primer coat on the entire eyelid from brow to lash edge.

2. Put a sunscreen (tinted) SPF 15 or higher on the entire face before makeup powder or cream; including ear tops and chest before going outdoors for long periods of time.

3. Always wash makeup off before bed, no exceptions.

4. False eyelashes for a more dramatic look for special events or stage.

5. Line lips with pencil or cream (aging diminishes the outline of lips).

6. Line eyebrows with pencil (eyebrow hairs can become thinner).

7. Daily astringent or clarifying product for removing any bacteria or dead skin on face using cottonball.

8. Exfoliate face and neck every week, facial mask every month.

Women Become Less Tolerant At Fifty Plus

We become less tolerant of others and others' children as well as other people's animals as we age. We become more forgiving of who we like and less forgiving of those we don't like or we don't know. This is human nature, but it intensifies when we get older and begin dealing with menopausal symptoms. Intolerant people are very unpopular people overall. Nobody wants to be around an intolerant, judgmental person. Partly hormonal, but you can't blame it completely on this one hormonal factor as we also have tendencies to become like our parents. The phrase "we become our parents" is so true with our core value and our upbringing developing our likes and dislikes. Attitude is everything, and how we react and adjust to something has already been established from our upbringing. What we can barely tolerate is vital to our happiness or unhappiness. It's very hard to adapt when we know from experience how something will play out and we struggle to listen to anything other than what we think we know. We form our opinions and then spend our entire lifetime validating what we believe to be true. This rigidity is sad, because there is so much we can learn from points of view that are different from our own. It takes an enormous amount of stress and stubbornness to keep our heart and mind closed to everything. A closed mind is always fighting to keep everything and everyone at arm's length. But we can learn a lot even as we age, and if we keep our minds open to new ways, thoughts, experiences, and other people's perspective, it will allow us to grow. We become very stagnant in our own ideas. You or your partner may sometimes feel that you never have all the information you want, but ask yourself, Do I have the information I need? There was a story about Henry Ford and the importance of getting information before making a decision.

Henry Ford was interviewing three individuals for a position as national manager for his company. After he took three regional managers to dinner, he soon chose one man to be his national manager. When the man later asked him why he had been chosen, Ford replied, "You had all been successful at selling, but you were the only one who tasted your food before you salted it. I like a manager who gets information before making his decision."

Making Decisions

It takes less time to make a better decision than it does to correct a poor decision.

A Story

A husband and wife had never been to a bed-and-breakfast before. They have been on cruises and lots of different hotels and lots of camping but never tried a bed-and-breakfast. Without ever experiencing it firsthand, the husband informed the wife, "It is just like staying with a friend for the weekend and having dinner and breakfast with them." Now how could the husband have any idea what it was like since he had never experienced a bed-and-breakfast? It is a perception that he had imagined and created so that there would be no need to explore it or try it out. He had already decided what it was like.

This is the rut we must avoid. Our close-minded friends and family members are welcome to verbalize their opinions, but *verify any information* that you receive for yourself. We should always make a practice of verifying information so we remove the risk of manipulation and missed opportunities. Ruts will spread into other areas of our life if we are not carefully paying attention. Make a practice to stay away from negative, close-minded people.

No company Is Better than Bad Company

If we keep bad people in our lives there will be no room for good people. It is a hard-driving world we live in today, and we must be willing to accept and tolerate others but not at our own expense. Be with people who have a similar work ethic to yours and who are passionate about making a difference, not so much financially powerful to make a difference, but involved in helping and inspiring other people. We are not on this earth merely for ourselves and our selfish needs and desires. We are rewarded for what we do to make someone else's life better here on earth. We will have better things happen to us when we have this spirit of living and giving. I guess some may consider it as karma, but I want to believe it is God making the pathway clear for us. As a reward for our happy spirit, we are blessed. Our lives are shaped by decisions that we do not think are all that important at the time. But our decisions work like dominoes. The results of one decision can affect the next decision more than we realize, and we need to be aware of this fact. There are people in our lives who may try to steal our joy, and you don't realize they are even doing it. The dominoes will start falling the wrong way if we are not careful to stop it. Further chapters will reveal how our thinking and attitude directly affect the outcome of our lives and our happiness.

While I have studied and researched many personality disorders, it appears that some are not obvious, and some become more apparent and intense as we grow older. This can be due to a trauma that occurred in our lives as children or adolescence or even self-esteem issues as adults due to a divorce, death of a loved one, or another stressful situation. These many traumas change our behavior as a self-protection, creating brain chemistry to change and resulting in disorders that are clearly evident. Any practiced behavior can become habits of living and eventually morph into who we are. You may have experienced this, or someone you know or love may have experienced the following changes. It is important to pay attention closely to these changes so we do not allow it to continue or reward bad behavior, sanctioning it to develop through time and practice. This could be you or someone you know.

DAMP People

I have developed an acronym for these types of people to avoid! I call them DAMP people!

- D—Double-crosser
- A—Attacker
- M—Manipulator
- P—Pretender

People who develop personality disorders don't come from an identical background or get to be who they have become based on similar experiences. If these type of people were to go to a mental-health professional for evaluation, they would not all have the same diagnosis and would instead be scattered across several different categories. Some would be diagnosed as antisocial personalities, some borderline personalities, and some paranoid personalities. Some might be considered oppositional defiant personalities, and some may fit into multiple categories.

Pay attention to people in your life and make good decisions to keep them in your life unless they demonstrate the tendencies that are going to be described. If they exhibit the traits, you must run from them as fast as you can.

These people (DAMP people) believe the end justifies the means. My mother would use that phrase all the time when she would notice and point out someone who was taking advantage of a situation in order to advance themselves regardless of who they hurt! They are totally self-focused and results oriented, and are willing to do anything to achieve their goal. They lack empathy and cannot identify with anyone else's emotions. They lack a conscience. They lack the ability to feel remorse, and they selfishly and narcissistically pursue whatever their own egos demand. They are consciously and subconsciously unscrupulous and will do anything it takes to get closer to their goal.

Sometimes you actually *help* them hurt you. If you are like most people in the world, you're probably not sure exactly what it is that you deserve.

We create our own experiences; we make our own breaks, because God gave us the gift of free will and we have to be responsible with it. The old saying "To whom much is given, much is expected." God gives us opportunities and allows obstacles to confront us, and we have to rise to the challenge. We must be trusted with what we have and prove we can handle ourselves before we are trusted and blessed with more. Our life is a reflection of good or bad decisions. Who we keep company with is an important decision.

Old Joke

A man was caught in a terrible flood situation in his town, and all the neighbors went running for high ground. The man said, "No, I'm staying here—God will save me." Eventually the flood forced him to his rooftop. The rescuers came by in their boat begging him to get aboard, one boat after another trying to help him. He said, "No, I'm staying here—God will save me." Finally, when the tide rose above the rooftop, and as he was floating in the water, he yelled at the heavens, "God, I kept the faith. I thought you were going to save me!" Then the clouds opened up, and he heard a booming voice say, "Hey, I sent you nine neighbors and three rescue boats. What else do you want from me?"

We are expected to use common sense. By gathering information it is our obligation to use our past experiences to base a decision on. If there are elements in your life that are missing, it is not always because of what someone did *to* you or didn't do *for* you. It is often because of what you do or don't do to create and claim what you wanted or needed.

If you aren't naturally a mean person and don't approach people and situations looking for an opportunity to take advantage, it's very hard to recognize that mind-set in others. Don't be naïve about DAMP people. If we don't have it within ourselves, we can be quite blind to it.

Here are some identifying characteristics that are typical for DAMP people.

- *They are arrogant and ruled by their own needs and desires.*

  Other people's needs just aren't real to them. You may approach a situation to enjoy it, learn from it, or just for the sake of doing it. A DAMP person is always looking for a way to capitalize on it, take advantage of it. A sense of entitlement is who they are. Their attitude is "this is mine…you just have it currently." Additionally you will see them indicate they don't appreciate a point of view other than their own.

- *They lack empathy and are incapable of feeling remorse or guilt and don't learn from their mistakes.*

  They do not have the ability to feel guilt or sorrow. They have a hidden agenda and no feelings about it at all. They don't even think they make mistakes. They sometimes will start therapy when required but don't have the self-awareness to benefit and are so narcissistic they can't get outside of themselves. They keep the same behavioral patterns and make the same mistakes over and over.

- *They are irresponsible, self-destructive, and disregard the well-being of others.*

  To them *everyone else* is a fool, but they never are themselves. A DAMP person is accident prone, but self-inflicted because they don't follow the rules or use common sense. They are often substance abusers.

- *They thrive on drama and crisis.*

  They love conflict and controversy. It accompanies them seemingly at every turn. They *need* drama, so they *create* it. They stir things up and love to see everyone getting upset. They love the power to make people react. They thrive on a good fight. They never learned the lesson of asserting their rights that it's not okay to be aggressive and trample on other people's rights. They have a low tolerance for frustration, a low threshold for engaging or exhibiting aggression, and poor impulse control.

- *They brag about outsmarting other people.*

  They believe they are not being dishonest; they are being smarter. They brag about screwing their partner over and believe everybody else should see it their way.

- *They have a pattern of short-term relationships.*

  They can't sustain a relationship because they have nothing to give, although they give the illusion of giving, maybe even over giving, to make you feel indebted. It's nothing but a way to make themselves look wonderful. Eventually people get what they give, and the relationship can't last.

- *They live in a fantasy world marked by delusion.*

They see themselves as victims or some exalted status. They are condescending toward others but may attempt to *hide* their contempt. They can turn to aggression to defend themselves.

These are the characteristics of a DAMP person who will infect your life and help you in no way except to make bad decisions and keep you from being happy. Your instincts should tell you that there are people out there and probably in your life who are not okay. Listen to your inner voice. Now that you are retiring, you don't have to let everyone into your life in the *same way*. Your job or career may have required you to endure company that is uninvited, but you can have differing levels of trust, appropriate to your level of involvement with people now. You need to believe in social sensitivity. Most people have a sense of social sensitivity. We read our audience. Are they bored and want to change subjects, confused, frustrated? Tuning in to this vibe is social sensitivity. DAMP people have no sensitivity to awkwardness of their aggressive pitch at a social function, have repeated conflict with colleagues, constant drama, personally and professionally, and publicly belittle others to magnify themselves. These DAMP people are already in your life right now, maybe as close as the person sitting next to you on your couch. This does not mean to be cynical or judgmental of people, but pay attention to observable information to determine a required level of self-protection. Watch the people in your life who manage your money, your family, your reputation. This is not about being paranoid; it is being vigilant and aware. So now you know that you need to spot them. You have the tools and identifiers to see them coming and avoid them.

We tend to *believe* people who we like; we also tend to like those who like us! One of the most powerful tools that a DAMP person will use is to make you feel liked by them, will flatter you, laugh at your jokes, agree with your positions, and support your efforts. If all you are ever hearing is what *you want to hear*, be afraid. Be very afraid. Don't get sucked into a conspiratorial relationship. If they worship you or put you on a pedestal and hold you in such high esteem, even if it's phony, they can eventually have a radical and extreme change of heart. You will wind up with an overzealous enemy.

- A DAMP person is too focused on getting your approval—as though their very existence depends on your accepting them. They are terribly insecure. They need you to endorse their position, whatever it may be, and they will use you to validate them at some point.

- A DAMP person cannot engage in a normal back-and-forth conversation or exchange, because they are too busy thinking about what information they can obtain for leverage. They may give the appearance of being engaged. Always answering a question with a question.

- A DAMP person will frequently avoid responding directly to any discussion that requires them to take a personal position. This narrows their ability to flip-flop. They also will take an irrelevant direction. This is a tactic to obfuscate by focusing on irrelevant details and answering questions that weren't asked.

- The DAMP individual will not take accountability or ownership for anything of negative consequence. This is a problem because people cannot change what they don't acknowledge. If the DAMP person acknowledges *nothing, they* change *nothing*. You cannot expect these individuals to hold themselves to a higher standard. It is not going to happen, and if you are in their life, you will become a target of blame. When they are not to blame, guess what, that leaves only *you*!

- A DAMP person loves to give you a false picture of reality through three types of misdirection— affirmative misstatements ("I saw him doing it"), lies by omission (failing to tell you what he saw), or half truths ("I saw him, but he had permission to do it")—knowing full well he gave a false picture of the situation. They pay attention to what you seem to respond to the most. They can gain credibility to their story by using you as a pawn.

- The DAMP individual will strive for imbalance, and they achieve this by overdoing for you, going way out of their way for you, so you are in their debt. If any relationship is too one-sided, you should be wary. You are being set up. They will try to convince you that "but for them" you would be miserable. Without them you would be lost, alone, incompetent, and downtrodden. Many husbands have, behind closed doors, convinced their abused wives that no one else would ever want her, love her, or even let her stay around. The early helpfulness and giving were never genuine and quickly become control and demand.

Bernie Madoff is a tragic example. He gained people's trust and purse strings. He took liberties with their money and destroyed many hardworking people's retirements and lives. Power corrupts and absolute power corrupts absolutely! Passive-aggressive sabotage is on the all-star hit list for DAMP people. They love this because they can do it and not get their hands dirty. They throw you under the bus and then say…what?

We can see in others only that which we possess within ourselves. That is why this chapter is so important. We do not have this DAMP (double-crosser, attacker, manipulative, pretender) attitude. We must be aware and watch for it. It can be very subtle and show its ugly head after years of being with a person.

Genetic factors may be a reason for the behavior of people who fit the DAMP profile. Unfortunately, the research is inconclusive. The root of the behavior is complex. Genetic factors have likely been reinforced by a number of environmental factors including parent modeling over the years. Children learn what they live. "If a child grows up with a parent who takes pride in 'beating the system' or constantly cutting corners, taking advantage of friends and acquaintances or even outright committing crimes then the child uses those behaviors as a reference point," says Dr. Phil McGraw in his book *Life Code*. "The most powerful role model in any child's life is the same-sex parent, so if sons watch their fathers cheat, abuse, and exploit, they are at high risk of following that pattern." By the time these DAMP individuals reach adolescence after being exposed to poor modeling, they've learned that all the patterns of behavior we have identified will help them get what they want. This is why they are resistant to therapy. Don't be fooled. Sometimes people who are the most articulate in the language of therapy are just using it to advance their own interest. It is just one more tool in their arsenal of manipulation. It gives the illusion of insight. Actions speak louder than words. Don't be a target!

Here are the DAMP tendencies:

- Very immature
- Seek immediate gratification
- No lasting relationship
- No sense of peace only drama
- So narcissistic they believe they are smarter than everybody else
- No real friends
- Admit to being lonely

Finally, I must warn you if you have friends or family members or you are struggling with DAMP tendencies, get counseling and don't allow the behavior! If the person grows older with these mean, obnoxious tendencies, imagine how lonely and isolated they will be when they are very, very old. It will take years of work and reforming new habits and modifying behavior with a conscious effort for these individuals to become socially and emotionally in tune with the world and others. They don't even realize what has happened! If you always allow them to be right, or take their unreasonable side just to shut them up, or pretend you weren't embarrassed when they called you a terrible name publicly and loudly because you did something they "didn't like," all this does is allow these behaviors to seem okay, and the behavior will continue. You are feeding into a lie. If you love the person and want to have them as part of your life, at least remove yourself from them and if possible explain why you must remove them from your life. A DAMP person may not want to think about their behavior and change it or even seek help, but at least you will know you used honesty and did them a favor by not accepting the inappropriate behavior. They will need to find someone else to push their DAMP tendencies on because it won't be you! The decision that is important to make is what level of effort is necessary to be happy after understanding these disorders and personality traits. Sometimes the squeeze isn't worth the juice from the orange. The amount of effort may be too great for the level of return. To be happy in your retirement years is a great return.

There is one more personality character that is neither DAMP or sociopathic type. It is called the misogynist man!

Misogynistic Husbands

"If he has the capacity to be so wonderful, then it must be something I am doing that's making things go wrong." If this is how we think about our husbands and the relationship, be careful. The misogynist bolsters this belief by reminding you that he would always be nice if only *you would* stop this or change that or be more of this or a little less of that. This is dangerous logic. You have leaped from recognizing that there are troublesome aspects to your partner's behavior to attempting to justify them or explain them away to now internalizing and accepting the responsibility for how he acts. I've heard women say, "Anytime I don't jump to his every command, he'd say, 'You're selfish, you don't know how to give in a relationship.'" Not all misogynists are as explosively critical. They express disappointment in quieter, more subtle ways. Comments such as how ridiculous your taste is and anyone with half a brain would know that. Glaring looks of disgust and condescension are equally as devastating.

Before delving into *why* a man may become misogynistic, we need to acknowledge *how* they manipulate and finally how to counteract this behavior successfully. It may be that the behavior has become so much of the man's overall character that no matter how you correctly respond and correct the behavior, it may be too late. This can be a critical crossroad decision. This is why it is important to understand the symptoms and actions that create this misogynistic manner. How women behave and respond will decide how happy or unhappy they will likely many years down the line be. Because it was not curtailed early on, the misogynist man may not *want to* or have the *ability* to change his behavior, so you may come to the conclusion that you need to take yourself out of the equation and let him ruin someone else's life instead.

It Is All About Control

The misogynist can get very mad over virtually nothing. He can explode over the most insignificant events. If he feels you have let him down in simply forgetting to pick up dry cleaning, or lettuce, run out of laundry soap, or toast is too dark, it is merely an opportunity to maximize it and make a mountain out of a molehill. Sadly, while accepting his attack and reducing *his* responsibility for it, she maximizes her failure, minimizing his behavior.

First Rule—Observe your partner. Pay close attention. The next time your partner attacks you, try to notice exactly what is happening to you. Then as quickly as possible sit down and make up a list of your reactions, emotional and physical reactions (i.e., hands shaking, goose bumps, sweating, etc.) Say to yourself, "Every single time he attacks me, I feel…" Then write down what you recall. When you write it down, it helps you clarify and focus. It creates distance and enables you to organize your thoughts and observe how you have been reacting all along for years. Observing your partner gives you the edge because he will now be predictable, which diminishes the intensity, and you won't be so panicked or surprised with his behavior.

You are supposed to read the mind of a misogynist and be all loving and adoring and nurturing. Idealization is a double-edged sword. It feels wonderful and flattering at first for you, but it also blinds a woman to the fact that it is impossible to be held up on a pedestal forever. The early indications of the misogynist's quick temper are sporadic. The explosions won't come and show their ugly head consistently until after a commitment has been made, such as moving in together or engagement. Then once he is sure he *has* her, the situation will rapidly change, so be careful in the dating pool and pay attention.

The next control weapons are (1) how his partner thinks, (2) how she feels, (3) how she behaves, (4) with whom and what she involves herself.

It is amazing how a successful, competent woman can disavow her own talents, needs and power in order to gain her partner's love and approval. Total control is impossible for any human being. So imagine how the misogynist is bound to fail miserably and become frustrated and angry much of the time. Sometimes he can mask his hostility, but other times it will manifest itself as psychological abuse.

Verbal Attacks

When anger is directed at you, it creates an atmosphere of tremendous tension. The shouting includes insults and attacks on you, and against your character or family's character. The misogynist will use anything necessary to get a reaction from you, including using familiarity and history for ammunition.

Some misogynists do not use scare tactics or screaming insults to gain control. They will wear down their partner by faultfinding and unrelenting criticism. This is a tricky way of control and disguise it as a way of teaching the woman how to be a better person or wife. The constant criticism and picking eats away at his partner's self-confidence and sense of self-worth.

Denial by convincing his partner the incident never happened, or reshaping the facts to fit the misogynist's version of it is common. Shifting the blame works to protect the misogynist man by convincing his partner that the problem is due to her and any questioning of him is immediately turned back around as further proving it is her inadequacies. This method of turning the tables helps deflect blame from themselves. One cruel statement can have much more impact than twenty positive ones. Verbal abuse has not been given the attention that it deserves, given how devastating it can be to a person's mental health over a period of time. I see it in my counseling practice every day. Recently, a client was recalling a special birthday party when she was turning thirty-five years old and how the gift her first husband gave her in front of her invited guests brought her to tears of humiliation. She broke down crying while relating the story. Sadly she has remembered this for almost twenty years!

How and Why Do Men Become Misogynistic?

One of the forces that drive the misogynist, we find that much of his abusive behavior is simply a way to cover up his tremendous anxiety about women. He is caught between his need for a woman's love and his deep-seated fears of her. His normal needs to be close to a woman are mixed with fears that she can annihilate him emotionally. His biggest fears are she will have power to hurt him, deprive him, engulf him, and abandon him. In an effort of protection, he *unconsciously* makes the woman in his life less powerful. Secretly he believes that if he strips her of self-confidence, she will be dependent on him as much as he is on her. By making her weak so she cannot abandon him, it calms his fears of abandonment.

While both parents raise a child, the mother is the nurturer, and the father helps pull the child away from the mother to prevent overdependence. The family background of misogynists is the opposite. The father is too timid or too passive to pull the boy away from the mother, so the boy has no option but to make the mother the center of his universe. The mother, instead of meeting the son's need with nurturing and comforting, is liable to get her son to meet *her* needs. Women in troubled marriages use their children to try to work out their problems. This is done by several ways—overwhelming demands, smothering control, or severe rejection. Regardless, the end result is the same. The boy becomes too dependent on her. In adulthood, he will transfer this dependency, causing conflict and fear onto the woman in his life. The misogynist saw his mother as having the power to frustrate him, to smother him, to withhold love from him, to make him feel weak, or make insatiable demands on him. He will now as an adult view his partner as possessing those same powers. If the father doesn't provide an alternative to his mother's influence, the son feels alone with his fears now. His panic and neediness make him vulnerable and drive him to behave in ways that counteract and protect themselves.

There are several other ways that can contribute to the misogynist's personality in adulthood. The father may already be a misogynist and may behave as a military officer and be extremely possessive and overbearing with his wife. The father was the unquestionable authority in the home. The behavior is parroted, and his thought may be "When I grow up, I'll get to scream and yell at everyone and treat people the way *I* want to, because that is what men get to do." The other option of being weak like his mother is not acceptable. By identifying with his father, he learned to tyrannize and abuse people. But the irony is if you look at the timid and sickly brother who lived in the home and never held a job now is in his thirties;he still lives at home with the mother, choosing to mimic the mother.

It's easy to understand how a boy learns from his misogynist father; however, boys with families where the father is passive and the mother is dominant and controlling may also be a misogynist. It is just as likely for a boy to become a misogynist if he has an overprotective mother who suffocates and over controls him. This type of mother will need to control everything and everyone in the family. She may do this by intruding in everybody's business. She is able to convince her boy that *she* is the only one that can handle or knows how to solve problems. This mother is likely to stay involved in their children's lives in adulthood as well. She cannot let her children grow up. She hovers over them and supervises their every move. We all know someone who has this tendency. By being so controlled, it prevents them from developing a sense of mastery over their own life. He doesn't have a chance to see himself as competent and effective because his mother will rush in and take charge, removing the opportunity. Every child should be able make mistakes and have room to try new experiences. When a child is unable to deal with his frustrations on his own with the mother swooping in and rescuing him from any discomfort, in adulthood he will be unable to handle even the most minor setback. The mother teaches the son you don't have to stand for frustration. Whatever happens, someone will be there to fix it, and finally it teaches that they are entitled to life without any irritation. This self-centered unhealthy entitlement attitude he has learned lets him believe that he can expect to always get whatever he wants when he wants it.

One's background directly affects how we become as adults. These deeply ambivalent feelings about women are based in large measure on their relationships with their mothers. We can see how men transfer these feelings onto the women with whom they become involved. He believes he is as dependent on his partner as he was on his mother. His terror of being alone, fear that she will leave him and being unable to cope or be overwhelmed by an insatiable neediness will grip him again when he is involved with his partner for life. Psychologically, he is still a frightened child.

How do we learn to love misogynist men? Understand that stress and anger or repressed rage can be one of the major sources of strain and damage to the body. If we don't face this head on it can actually begin to wear the body out. When women don't deal with their unacceptable rage at their partners, many women unconsciously redirect their anger inward, back on to themselves. The more a woman does this, the more it will show up manifesting itself mentally and physically. Medical and psychiatric literature is filled with illnesses that result from this inability to deal with emotional distress. Depression, body aches, muscle spasms, general body tightness, and /or tension headaches are a few. Many other cardiovascular and digestive tract issues such as colitis, chronic indigestion, and various types of bowel disorders can also be directly connected to expressions of stress.

Second Rule—Choose to continue to behave exactly as you have been. Many think that you need to change when dealing with a misogynist individual. Do exactly what you have been doing with one crucial difference: recognize that the choice to behave as they do is now theirs. Consciously plan something and carry it out, choosing to do it. You make yourself active, instead of reactive. Behavior you do out of fear or intimidation feels terrible; however, behavior done out of choice feels better. This is a big step, choosing the way you will react. This will desensitize your feelings of powerlessness in your relationship. You may choose to apologize for something, but you do not *have* to apologize. Sometimes I would wear earbuds listening to my iPod full of my favorite music while working on something by myself. Listen to music while doing a project. This will discourage any directive, controlling suggestions from your spouse when you are not asking for any help or input. (Sometimes it isn't even turned on, but he doesn't know that!) It's my Zen time. You may choose to use a suggestion he may offer, but you don't *have* to use a suggestion. No intimidation or ridiculing is allowed if you don't use a suggestion.

Third Rule—Change the way you see your partner. His behavior is not okay. His behavior has very little to do with you. Ask these questions:

1. Would any reasonable person get so upset over such a minor incident?

2. Does part of a loving relationship include constant criticism or correction or picking and blame shifting?

3. Is he just looking for an excuse to attack or ridicule me?

4. Is he blaming me for all those things he doesn't want to take responsibility for himself?

5. Does anyone have the right to treat another human being the way he is treating me?

These questions will help validate your inner perception of what is going on now, or if you were once in a relationship with a misogynist but no longer are. These questions will help you pay closer attention to the same behavior with other men in your future. It will be uncomfortable for you when you become aware of how unloving and unacceptable your partner's behavior is.

I would sometimes say to myself when my husband's behavior was juvenile, "What are you…a child?" This would allow me to really step back and see how ridiculous it was, taking the emotion out of it. We step away the same way when we are dealing with a young child throwing a temper tantrum ignoring the behavior.

Fourth Rule—Never call yourself a name, to yourself or to your partner. Things like, how could I have been so stupid? How could I have let this happen to me? I am so dumb! Don't add self-inflicted punishment to the punishment you are already experiencing.

Fifth Rule—Don't tell him off. Although it is certainly understandable to want to do this and a pattern of doing this may be typical, resisting and repressing this urge may be hard. The reason is because of the following:

- He is a master at winning with you.

- He is a master at changing the subject, rewriting history, and sidetracking.

- He will deny whatever is said.

- He will not "hear" you.

- He will blame you for everything as always.

- He will make you back down.

- He will use intimidation to get his way.

- Misogynists feel assaulted when their behavior is being confronted or challenged.

Sixth Rule—Stop feeding your partner's bad behavior. The characteristic way she handles his attacks can actually be feeding and reinforcing the bad behavior. Every time she defends herself, pleads with him, or becomes hysterical, she is being *reactive* rather than *active.* She will be doing exactly what he wants her to do. He overwhelmed her and made her helpless, which ultimately left him in control.

Seventh Rule—Start intentionally putting new phrases into your vocabulary. When your feelings and needs are not given consideration or respect, you must begin the difficult task of a new vocabulary.

- This is what I think.

- This is what I believe.

- This is what I will do.

- This is what I will not do.

- This is what I want.

Decrease your vocabulary of these phrases:

- I'm sorry.

- Is this okay?

- Do you agree with me?

- Do you like it?

- If you are going to get upset, I'll do what you want.

People who feel good about themselves are able to say, "I can tell you my opinion and let you like it or not like it." In a misogynistic relationship, only the misogynist's opinions are permitted.

Eighth Rule—Define what you want. Here is a list of things you may want. Create your own based on these below.

Things I want:

- I want respect.

- I want kindness.

- I want to be allowed to express myself.

- I want to be heard.

- I want the right to have my own beliefs and opinions.

- I want to be an equal partner in matters concerning money.

- I want my sexual needs to be as important as his.

- I want an equal voice in making decisions that affect both of us.

- I want respect for the work that I do (whether in or out of the house).

- I want us to participate in activities that are important to me, not just the ones you select.

Ninth Rule—Set your limits with your partner. Here is the challenge: changing your behavior with him. The behavioral changes are not difficult to learn and can greatly affect the power imbalance that is likely to exist in your relationship. It is easy to get caught up in an argument. But the very explosiveness and amount of the misogynist's anger is a signal that the anger is inappropriate to the subject at hand. The anger is about something else. *Non defensiveness* is a great tool here. In order to change your relationship, one of you has to start behaving like an adult. It's not likely to be your misogynistic partner. By using nondefense responses, you begin to set up a climate that is less explosive. It is essential to establish this climate before you can begin to set limits on his behavior.

New Assertive Statements

- It's not okay for you to talk to me this way.

- It is not okay for you to treat me this way.

- Screaming isn't going to work anymore.

- This is one time you can't intimidate me.

- I know that this has always worked before, but I want you to know it is not going to work anymore.

- I will not stand here and be screamed at.

- I will discuss the topic with you after you calm down.

- I will not accept being put down by you.

- You've controlled me in the past, but it isn't working anymore.

Rehearse these lines in front of a mirror. Repeat them until they come easily and feel natural. It should sound strong and natural.

Use the ability to think differently. The old thoughts will keep us stuck, but a new thought will free us. These new thoughts help us step back and keep us from being swept into the intense emotions of the moment. Do you remember your mother saying to you when you were young, "Sticks and stones may break my bones, but words will never hurt me"?

New Thoughts

- I'm an adult.
- Yelling can't destroy me.
- He's behaving like a spoiled brat.
- He's acting like a big baby.
- He's out of control.
- He's responsible for his behavior, not me.

Remind yourself that "who I am is not dependent on his opinion of me." Each time you act in a new way, it becomes easier for you. Results may not be immediate. Because the misogynist is unaware of how hurtful and abusive his behavior is, you will need to show him how to behave.

When he behaves especially nice to you, use these sentences to reinforce this behavior and teach him.

- I really appreciate it when you…
- It really makes me feel good when you…
- It was nice of you to…
- I love it when you…

Some misogynists will soften up and become friendlier once they see that they can't push you around anymore. If this happens, more closeness and equality can develop between you.

However, if it is time to leave, ambivalence after separation is very common. It is treacherous with the misogynist because his Jekyll and Hyde behavior enables him to be exactly the man you want him to be, but soon his controlling and demeaning behavior will reappear. It may even be worse because now he has added justification to get back at you for abandoning him.

Tenth Rule—Trust Yourself. You will know when it's time to leave. Hold on to the qualities that make you unique. Use your intuition and let go of self-denying behaviors. Being a woman no longer means to be passive, submissive, and self-denigrating. No one teaches you how to behave in a relationship, and you can clearly see how our upbringing and past behavior conditions us and can directly affect how we *treat* our spouses or *react* to our spouses.

All of us have a different level of tolerance. Some women have absolutely none and have been married several times looking for happiness. This chapter has clearly shown that others may have disorders that can easily contribute to our unhappiness. We can love ourselves enough to set limitations on how others should act and use our inner compass to gauge when it is going in the wrong direction. As the song goes by Madonna, "If they can't give me proper credit, I'll just walk away" ("Material Girl"). I recently started singing this song on stage with the bands that I play drums in.

We are in charge of our happiness even though we may be less tolerant in our fifties. We can be in control of our lives and make good decisions. The most important decision is to be happy.

When most of us make a decision, we do only one of two important things: we either use our heads or we listen to our hearts. But we seldom do both. So we often make half decisions based on half-truths.

Women Need to
Make Better Decisions

Using My Head

Three questions to ask yourself when making a decision, based on a book by Spencer Johnson MD.

Practical Question

- Am I meeting the real need?

- Am I informing myself of options?

- Am I thinking it through? What if?

Don't let your ego get in the way of your decision making. More often than we realize, the way to quickly arrive at better results is to get around the obstacle that is in our way. It is usually our *self!* Because more often than not, a person with character will make better decisions, especially a person with integrity, intuition, and insight. *Integrity*, because people who have integrity won't fool themselves about a situation. They will cut through the nonsense and get to the true core of things quickly. *Intuition*, because people who have learned to trust their intuition won't look to others to make their tough decisions, they depend on themselves. *Insight,* which is vital for eliminating self-sabotage.

Using My Heart

Private Question

- Does my decision show I am honest with myself?
- Does my decision show I trust my intuition?
- Does my decision show I deserve better?

The Yes or No System

I use my head by asking myself a practical question. I consult my heart by asking myself a private question. Then after I listen to myself and others, I make a better decision and act on it.

The next decisions you make in your normal way, stop for a minute and ask yourself a head question and a heart question. Everybody could use a better decision making system in today's changing world. We all need to make better decisions, faster, just to survive, let alone prosper. The better the system to make good decisions, the easier it will be to avoid mistakes and get consistently better results.

When using my head and asking the practical question, I will be making sure I am meeting the real need, informing myself of options and thinking it through.

It takes less time to make a better decision than it does to correct a poor decision. You realize that you usually do have options, often several options, but you may not be aware of them at that time. When you hear yourself say "*I have no other choice*," just smile at yourself. You are simply not aware of your options. Fear can paralyzed us, and "fear-frozen minds" sometimes think there is no other choice. So it is important to become aware of your options. You begin by asking questions and gathering needed information. Needed information is only what you actually need to know to make a better decision. Do not avoid what you do not want to hear, you will not be aware of all your real options. Don't be naïve. Validate the information yourself. What can you depend on more, someone else's words or your own eyes or ears? Fear fogs our vision.

Multitasking frenzy

We all get the same twenty-four hours, not one minute more or less in a day! What we do with that same twenty-four hours is based on our individual priorities and what gives us a sense of purpose. I believe that everyone needs a sense of purpose to be at peace. We can't just serve only ourselves in this fast-paced world and feel good at the end of a day. Women, as much as men, need to feel needed, important, and productive. Women always feel like there is just not enough time. How often do we try to do more than one thing at a time? It is great to be able to multitask, but it is difficult to be present-moment oriented. You not only lose out on much of the potential enjoyment of what you are doing, but you also become far less focused and effective. Many times we are speaking to someone, but our minds are somewhere else, while we are doing three or four chores all at the same time. Try to block out a period of time where you do only one thing at a time— whether you're washing dishes, talking on the phone, driving a car, playing with your child, talking to your spouse, or reading a magazine. Be present in what you are doing. Concentrate. Don't buy into the craziness of our frenzied society if you want peace. Turn off the radio and have quiet.

Contrary to popular belief, there is no such thing as multitasking. The brain can attend to only one thing at a time. Being too busy or not being busy is an interpretation of our activity. Being busy is a state of mind. Have you ever noticed that half an hour in the dentist's chair lasts longer than half an hour at a fun dinner party with friends? How about five minutes when you are on the phone placed on hold passes more slowly than five minutes watching a movie. Time is how we *live it*. The clock is supposed to work for us, not against us. Take three consecutive breaths slowly when feeling compulsive or driven. It is difficult to shake this habit of persistent mania of feeling task and time driven. Time is an internal, not external, reality. Don't allow yourself to feel like a prisoner of lists or being too busy. Be a person of excellence and do what you can handle well and have the strength to control how much you will do or accept. You are never too busy to go for a walk or go on an overdue trip to get away for a weekend.

Next time you are busy, ask yourself a question, if I was told I would only have a few years to live, whom would I call, and how much energy would I waste on things that didn't matter?

In a 2013 study, subjects who had eighteen weeks of talk therapy sessions had an average of 50 percent improvement in their digestive symptoms. They also experienced less mood and anxiety disorders. Taking the time to be mindful by cutting back on multitasking, in addition to the talk therapy will only keep you feeling in control of your life.

Eye of the Storm

Practice being in the "eye of the storm." The eye of the storm is that one specific spot in the center of a twister, hurricane, or tornado that is calm, almost isolated from the frenzy of activity. Everything around the center is violent and turbulent, but the center remains peaceful. How nice it would be if we too could be calm and serene in the midst of chaos—in the eye of the storm. It is much easier than you might imagine being in the eye of a human storm. What it takes is intention and practice. Start with family gatherings, cocktail parties, and birthday parties for children. You'll be more present-minded oriented. You'll enjoy yourself more than ever before. Practice listening. Let others be right and let them enjoy the glory. Once you have mastered harmless circumstances like these, you can practice on more difficult areas of life—dealing with conflict, hardship, or grief. If you start slowly you will have some success, then keep practicing. Pretty soon you'll know how to live in the eye of the storm. It will become such a habit that turmoil will not affect you and control you. Sometimes when we focus on who is to blame or deflecting blame, we can't stay in the eye of the storm. Most of the time it doesn't even matter and is pointless. Take deep breaths and be calm and stay in the eye of the storm.

Don't Sabotage Your Decision Making

Organization can really help you gain control in your life and get that feeling of frenzy and out of control anxiety to be less intense. We discussed organizing our lives and our homes using a filing system and streamlining in chapter 2. Let's acknowledge that we now have Facebook, e-mails, smartphones, and lots of technology to adjust to. We still have our chores and responsibilities, and some have grandkids. Some of us are still taking care of our aging parents or grandparents. The list goes on and on. Some days should be for just reading outside in the shade, or making cookies with the grandkids. Other days are meant for tasks and responsibilities. Where the problem lies is that we tend to procrastinate on things until it overwhelms us, instead of handling things as they occur and taking action instead of reaction. You must feel in control of your life and of your time to really have peace. We must tell ourselves what to do every day and what to prioritize.

Every day we wake up, we should create a plan, not just wing it. Generally people who plan things and have goals have less depression, suicide, and are happier people. They also have fewer car crashes, better credit, and have more self-control.

182

I used to instruct Nick, my son, to put on paper his list of chores for himself so he could tell himself what to do and what to prioritize. I would look in his room when he was a teenager and say, "What is wrong in your room?" I would not tell him what to do, even if it was clearly undone. He would have to figure out what it was and then tell himself to do it, merely by me asking a question instead of giving specific direction. Psychology 101 again!

A Story

There was a chicken coop full of chickens and an eagle was born among the chickens. As the eagle grew up, he became more and more like a chicken. He would eat like a chicken, peck like a chicken, and even walk like a chicken. One day he saw an eagle flying above in the sky and wished he could fly too. As he looked around, he saw other chickens, but somehow felt like he was meant to fly. He began noticing his wingspan was much larger than the other chickens' and soon decided to attempt to fly. The other chickens mocked him and laughed as he would crash into the chicken coop trying to fly. The chickens would say, "You are just a chicken, why are you even trying to fly?" The eagle would just ignore them and kept practicing over and over. He said to himself, *I don't think like a chicken, I don't look like a chicken, I don't feel like a chicken.* Then one day, while attempting to fly, he was lifted by the air current and began to soar like an eagle. He was never around chickens again.

We all have talent and ability that others may not recognize or understand. Don't listen to the others who are like chickens telling you that you'll never be able to do something. Good breaks and success come from those who don't listen to others but follow their desires and work hard for it. If you want it bad enough, you must keep thinking about what you want and with effort you will get it. You are what you think you are!

Maybe what is needed for good decision making is to reprioritize our lives. Decide what is important for each day and work on those items. Write them down and work on them all day. Designing a whole week of accomplishments can give you a sense of control. The feeling of accomplishment is incredible and makes you feel happy, at peace, and in control of your life. It will keep retirement more exciting too! Perhaps you do not always need to make the *best* decisions for things to be better, we only need to make *better* decisions. You will find that if you just keep making better decisions, eventually you will do well and have your desired results. Unresolved conflict or issue is the highest stressor we can have. Things undone are unresolved issues and we cannot have peace without addressing them. That gutter that is hanging off the roof has been like that for years or the half-completed project is unconsciously and subliminally causing stress. We talked about how stress and conflict creates more cortisol in your body, making you store more fat long after the stress has temporarily subsided. This will take years off your life. Now we have an additional stress because we now have more fat to fight!

Besides organizing and reprioritizing our lives, how can we survive this fast-paced lifestyle? We need a sense of peace.

Peace is achieved by being in control. Write down all the things you would love to do in your life without regard to money or freedom or circumstances. Take the list and then prioritize it in order of importance. Then pick a time frame for each two or three items and separate into five years or less, ten years or less, and so on.

To make a better decision, I first stop proceeding with a poor decision or what doesn't work. Although it is often dangerous, we feel safer if we do not change what is familiar. Eventually, the ineffective familiar way becomes accepted. You can see this clearly in private organizations.

An example of accepting ineffectiveness:

A Story

Many years ago, the US Army wanted to get off more rapid rounds of cannon fire, and so they hired a consultant to study the problem. He went into the field and noticed that the soldiers stepped back from the cannon and waited for about three seconds every time before they fired the cannon. When asked why, they replied that they were following directions laid down in the army manual. The consultant read through all the back issues of the manual until he had traced the instructions back to their origin in the Civil War. The soldiers were advised back then to step away from their weapons before firing so they could hold the gun horses' heads; otherwise, the horses would bolt, jerking the cannons off target, which were attached to the horses. When the soldiers realized this wasn't necessary any longer since horses were no longer used and this was only done out of a standard practice and comfortable habit, they of course finally changed it.

But how many of us are holding on to something that may not be working? It may feel comfortable and familiar, but we are missing out without even realizing it! If you wanted to drive west, and suddenly realized you were going east, what would you do? You would turn around and change directions as soon as you realized it. Our making better decisions to have more peace in our lives involves us going in a better direction, making different decisions and priorities that may be out of our comfort zone. I recently heard about a very sad father's comment following the suicide of his twenty-year-old daughter. He said, "Think of all the choices she didn't see she had." The saddest part is that what frightens us and paralyzes us is usually *not* real. When you find out what *is* real by gathering information, you are aware of the alternative you have had all along. There are two kinds of information, information that is *nice to have* and information that you *need to have.*

One of the first steps to arriving toward a better decision is, yes, *to stop.* When I don't know how to say yes to a better decision, I can first say no to a poor decision and stop doing what doesn't work. Even if you do not know a better way, you will most likely fill this void that is created with something better. Using my heart asking a private question, I ask, does my decision show I am honest with myself? Trust my intuition? Deserve better? I've learned that the reason most of us have problems is that we fool ourselves. Integrity is telling myself the truth. Honesty is telling the truth to other people. When we have to hide from the truth, we feel more frightened.

A Story

Years ago, there was a television ad for motor oil that showed a garage mechanic with a can of oil, saying, "You can pay me a little money now." Then the advertisement showed the mechanic removing the car's engine and saying, "Or you can pay me a lot more money later."

The advertisement was promoting how changing the oil in your car was important. It is necessary to add motor oil to my car whether I like it or not. The fiction is, you can get away with not spending the time or money to put oil in your car and it will still all work out just fine. But the reality is that your engine will eventually burn out. And it doesn't matter if you believe you need to add oil or not. It is like the people who believed long ago that the earth was flat. The earth was nevertheless round, regardless of what the people believed. Believing it was flat did not make it flat. Believing in an illusion doesn't make it true. Poor decisions being based on our illusions will not turn out well and most times make matters worse. You must admit that when you look back on a poor decision, you can see sometimes where you just fooled yourself. Other people usually see our mistakes more easily than we do, and often you can see theirs. If you think you are blind to your illusions, you may find help from the people who care about you. If they are all saying the same thing in various ways, then you can hear them; acknowledge it and make changes. It's your ego that hangs on to your illusions. *When* we make our decision is as important as *what* we decide to do. In this day and age, we all need to make better decisions sooner.

A Story

Some hikers were on a hike with a guide and came across an ice bridge. The guide makes it clear that if they wait, the sun could warm the ice, weaken the bridge, and endanger their crossing. They need to act soon, not wait until the situation is worse. "The truth is, the sun *is* going to melt the ice, whether you see the truth of this or not" said the guide.

Our perception doesn't affect the reality. As a metaphor we need to look at whatever "the melting ice" is in our own decisions and deal with it soon. When we live in illusion, we look to others like an ostrich that buries its head in the sand. While we ignore the sun overhead, the once-solid ice bridge melts out from under us.

The word *intuition* means being "in tuition." *Tuition* comes from the Latin verb *tueri*, meaning "to watch over." In medieval times, *tuicion* meant "protecting." Today it means teaching. Your intuition protects by teaching, based on what has worked in the past and what is most likely to work now. To use your intuition, it is important to look at how you feel as you are making your decision. If you make a decision, it manifests as "feeling a lot of effort," you are probably trying to force things to happen. If so, it will probably turn out poorly for you. You should feel peaceful. Intuition includes not only what you feel about the decision but also what you sense. Are we making decisions with fear or enthusiasm? Remember the word *enthusiasm* comes from the Greek *entheos*, which means "the God within." So we think with our minds and feel with our bodies. Our minds can become confused, but our bodies speak to us in a simple binary code: either "Yes, things feel right to us" or "No, they do not feel right." Listen to your gut and trust it. Lastly, when you make a decision, even though you probably think it is illogical, could it be that you do not believe you deserve any better? Could your decisions reflect your sabotaging belief, even though you are unaware of it? The word *deserve* comes from the Latin word *deservire*, meaning "to serve zealously." But how many of us deserve what is really in our better interests zealously? You may think you deserve better, but not really believe it or act on it. Make sure you are not avoiding information you know you need. You deserve that! The sad truth is we often get the results we unknowingly believe we deserve.

We also tend to be subconsciously in competition with others around us. Running you own race is difficult to do sometimes when we are busy watching others. Our relatives or friends may have a nicer car or nicer house than we do. They are running their race the way they want, and we need to resist the temptation to run our race in direct competition with what others are doing. Using an analogy of a racetrack at a car race, your friend or relative could be spending money and running their race down a dirt road that will become windy and may go off a cliff that they cannot yet see! You don't want to judge them or follow them because it is their race and you have your own road that may be rocky and difficult to pay attention to. It is easy to fall into the trap of wanting more or looking better with a fancy car or wardrobe. But don't be caught up making your decisions in your life following others or competing with others. We are not sheep. The domino effect hasn't *yet* caused a catastrophic result. For others and their decisions, they are solely based on their own personal circumstances. Base your decisions and actions on your *own* circumstances without regard to others. Don't keep up with the Joneses because the Joneses *may* be worse off than you know. Later, when they turn seventy years old and have regrets, it will be too late to change the direction of their life and future consequences. It just hasn't happened yet. Run your own race. Do what is good for you and your family circumstances. Many people spend their entire life indefinitely preparing to live! Many also spend their entire lives secretly competing with others.

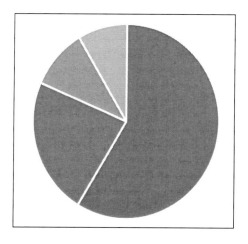

Make Your Pie of Life

Each slice of your pie represents what you do in your life and how much time is spent, which is reflected by how large the slice is. If you make a pie reflecting your life and priorities now, it may be evident how large some slices are. You may want to change the percentage of time you give to some items or areas of your life. A husband and wife can both make a pie of life and live under the same roof, and you would be shocked when you look at the pie slices. You would think they were not living in the same house with the same circumstances. Now the trick is to create a pie of life as you would like it to be! Ask your significant other to do the same and I can assure you that your pies will look completely different. Men will have food and sex as a large slice of this pie of life. Women may have laundry, shopping, or pampering themselves as large slices. We all need to create a large slice of the pie with an activity that gives the dopamine rush in the same way as sugar or any pleasurable activity provides. This will allow balance and happiness for a full well-rounded life.

Ultimately you will make the decisions as to what is in your pie of life and how big a slice each area will be. You make your own happiness when you make your pie of life. This will help open the conversation with your spouse as well by matching up similar likes in your pie of life. Retirement creates a different pie of life than while you are working. After retirement it is very smart to begin with a pie of life chart to look at and discuss in order to be moving in a similar direction.

Women Need to Embrace Menopause

You can only control yourself, not the other person you are around or married to. If you watch Dr. Phil on TV, you know that this is something he talks about all the time. We must ignore what we can't control. A teenager who is doing drugs—we can lead a horse to water, but we can't make them drink. A marriage that is long term and going nowhere with too much water under the bridge, or too much poison poured on it, can only be controlled by what we do individually. The weather may be turning bad and raining even though we planned a camping trip. We can't control the weather or other individuals or things in our lives, but we can devise a plan B or plan C to make it work out better.

Ignore what is not in our power to change and change only our own attitudes and focus on ideas to adapt. This allows us our happiness through the stormy situation. You can't control what you cannot see! Fear and faith have something in common. They both ask us to believe something will happen that we cannot see! It has not happened yet.

Fear says believe the negative!

That pain in your side is the same thing your grandmother died from. It'll be cancer and the death of you!

Faith says believe the positive!

That pain in your side is probably from the extra-long baseball game you played the other day.

When negative thoughts come in, don't let them take root. Switch to a faith-minded attitude. Don't use your energy to worry. Use your energy to believe. It takes the same amount of energy to believe as it does to worry. You can control your future.

Our Menopausal Brain

The amygdala, pronounced (a mig da la), is a part of the brain. It is activated when there is stress. It activates cortisol and epinephrine during stress. The brain can't distinguish between a tiger running after you or "nobody loves me" feeling. When the body is in stress, the repair mechanisms are disabled. An animal will relax in ninety minutes after stress. Humans endure fifty stresses per day. This means when you have a relationship struggle, experiencing loneliness, miserable work environment, financial worries, or other anxiety, your brain cannot relax. You have to eat a lot of kale to counterbalance any stress you endure in a day.

Some think that stressfulness all the time means they are busy and worth more because they are busy. Stressfulness represents that they must be important if they are constantly going one hundred miles per hour every day. It becomes normal! For menopausal women it can be disastrous to our bodies. It can cause physical pain in joints. Our aging bodies need calcium and other nutrients now more than ever. Seventy-five percent of women experiencing physical symptoms such as abdominal pain or problems, can be traced back to an emotional issue or trauma they experienced at a young age. When the body is in stress mode continuously, your amygdala part of your brain cannot rest. It sends a fight or flight message to your entire body. Your body is strong but fragile. If we identify and pay attention to our bodies and our inner voice and feelings, we can balance the ratio of relaxation responses to stress responses.

An exercise to do next time you have a big crisis: slowly breathe normally and say a short sentence on the exhale—for example, "I feel calm," "I am relaxed," "My day will be peaceful," or "I love my life." Repeat this five times, and every time your mind wanders, bring it back to the sentence and push the distractions or the thought away. You may need to do this after the crisis has passed to bring your brain back to a calm place. Losing your keys when you are already late or anything that creates anxiety or frantic feeling can benefit from this exercise. Driving to your appointment running late would be a good time to do deep breathing exercises, giving you back control. When you arrive to your destination, you will be more relaxed.

Other things you can do to calm the amygdala part of your brain are playing with animals, dancing, yoga, gardening, praying and attending religious services.

When I run in the mornings in my neighborhood or to downtown Tacoma, I am *not* thinking about our finances, my relationships, my jobs or responsibilities. I am thinking about the music on my iPod, looking at the city view, feeling my body move. This is so my brain has a half hour or more to relax.

Negative thoughts make you more vulnerable to anxiety and depression. Women are more prone to depression than men. Blood flow to the brain goes down during menopause and could be why there are more memory issues and depression for women during menopause.

Progesterone—Relaxes you

Estrogen—Helps you think clearly

We start losing progesterone ten years before we go into menopause. That's the relaxing hormone. Then when our estrogen goes way down during menopause, we notice we can't think clearly.

Feeding the brain with a positive mental attitude and doing relaxation techniques when you are stressed will make a big difference if you practice it regularly.

Adding DHA and EPA supplements along with some sort of exercise is bound to make a difference as well. A woman's brain has 52 percent more active matter than a man's brain. We have so much going on that it is overwhelming to our brains. If we are not storing a reserve of nutrients to heal our brains, we are more vulnerable to depression, physical ailments, increased weight, Alzheimer's, and ultimately unhappiness in how we look and feel.

Studies show omega 3, which is in DHA, increases your brains ability to make new cells. It turns on the gene to grow new brain cells. We were always told as young kids you don't grow new brain cells. But studies have shown that exercise helps turn on genes to grow new brain cells and a 60 percent to 70 percent reduction in Alzheimer's. With DHA omega 3 the risk for Alzheimer's is fifty-fifty. The DHA talks to your DNA in your body and tells it to increase your brain ability to make new cells.

EPA is fish oil that helps with attention deficit disorder. As we age, the brain is less and less active, and this can help boost the reserve in your brain.

Our genes are influenced by the lifestyle choices we make. Every food product we consume, the amount of exercise we get or don't get, the amount of sleep, and amount of stress directly contribute to the expression of our DNA. We *can* change the expression of our DNA. We are in control of our genetic destiny. It is not all written in stone.

Isolation can make you feel depressed. Our brains need stimulation, not television stimulation unless you are watching paid television or a music channel and learning a musical instrument by observing. Positive and negative are handled by different areas of the brain. Negative memory takes up more space in the brain than positive memory. We tend to remember more negative than positive if we don't train our brains to change that habit. An example would be when we lose $75 dollars. We will remember that much longer than gaining $75 dollars. The negative has more impact. You can get ten compliments and be on cloud nine and then get one negative comment and you only believe and think about that one negative comment. We need to train our brains to not choose to focus on the negative. To say no when we watch negative things on television or beat ourselves up for a bad choice or failure, remembering only what you did wrong for future decisions. Learning to resist the emotional drama of replaying a negative thing is difficult and takes telling yourself what to do. Verbalizing it out loud gives it more power because your brain will obey your words. If you continue to be negative and dwell on the negative and feel bad about things, never healing, then you are choosing to ruin your life and happiness.

An example would be like a scab that is trying to heal. If you keep picking at it when it is trying to heal, then it has to start all over again, creating another scab, and continues on and on.

- *The Stress of Fear*

    Living in *fear* is like running from the tiger all the time, and it is hard on the amygdala part of your brain. It doesn't know the difference between fears of falling or fear of dwindling finances or fear of a cancer diagnosis.

- *The stress of availability*

    The stress of being available all the time, which includes errands, favors for others, or instant reachability on the cell phone has begun to create an anxiety. When we forget our phone it is a catastrophe! When we can't reach someone by cell phone, we blow up their phone until they answer. The anxiety it causes the person pursuing as well as the person ignoring is incredibly hard on your body, hormones, and the amygdala portion of your brain.

- *The Stress of Unforgiveness*
  Unforgivingness and bitterness will also cause the amygdala of your brain and your body to undergo stress. People who feel guilty because they cannot forgive or will not forgive are not very happy and no one wants to be around them. Remember negative memory takes up more space in the brain than positive memory. Such a waste of brain memory! Here is a way you can think of letting go of things like bitterness, resentment, abandonment or hurt.

Example:
   You throw away something in the garbage can in the kitchen, then you take it out to the large container outside. On garbage day you walk the garbage can out to the curb of your street and it gets picked up by the city garbage collectors who then take it to the dump site. Would you go to the dump site to take back a piece of garbage?

This is how you think about letting go of something that is past garbage, past hurt, past bad decisions. Letting go is like throwing away the garbage and never seeing it again. There will always be new garbage, but empty out the garbage in your life and let go and let your brain relax. Your body will follow what your brain says to do. The only past garbage to think about is a few pieces to learn from and not make the same mistakes repeatedly. You accomplish nothing by digging through garbage of your past, especially while you are more emotional during menopause to begin with. If you rethink and relive the garbage of your past, like hurt or humiliation, you unknowingly will naturally take it out on those around you like your friends, family, and future relationships.

Design Your Own Retirement

- Think about how you want to spend your retirement and make a pie chart of the amount of time you want to devote to travel, working, gardening, etc., similar to the pie of life in the earlier chapter. You may find your retirement pie may be very different than your spouse's. You may want to do this pie of retirement before you retire. Personally I can tell you that if I had done this pie with my husband, our pie would be very different. He would have larger slices that wouldn't even exist in my pie at all. That being said, the earlier you get this pie chart figured out, the easier it will be to go on vacations together after retirement. Day-to-day living can be enough of a challenge while you spend all day together.

- Make a wish list of things you haven't done yet but want to do, then prioritize the list and work with your financial advisor to set aside the money you'll need for those "must do's." Ladies, give yourself permission to have a "must do."

- Talk to your financial advisor before you retire. Your financial situation will determine some of what your retirement looks like, including what you can and can't expect to do. You may each only be able to pick one thing. Don't throw up your hands and give up your dream or a "must do" just to agree to something that only your spouse would enjoy. There is always room to compromise.

- Check Social Security rules because you may be able to collect your spouse's SS while your spouse is still continuing to work. If it is under the maximum yearly income guidelines, this allows your spouse's Social Security to continue to grow, while the wife collects if she meets the age criterion. It's worth a phone call to your Social Security office. Things change all the time. This would be information you *need to know* from my chapter on making good decisions based on information you acquire. An effort of a phone call can sometimes come back to you in savings over and over again.

- Budget now and plan to have your debt ratio low, paying off cars credit cards, etc. This will make your lifestyle more affordable later

when you don't have a full- or part-time job.
Simply stop buying large items, throw away
the old, and purchase and replace only what
you will use in your retirement years. There
is a point where your mind-set will change as
you age. Everybody's mind-set changes some
are just slower or faster than others. Your son
can now have the chain saw your husband will
never use again—for example, an older washer
and dryer that you removed out of a rental
that you can now give to someone instead of
storing in the garage as a backup. There is a
time when you don't need a backup. Watch
the show "Hoarders" on television and see
the results of not changing your mind-set for
retirement. If you have been budgeting, you can
begin replacing things you may need to own
in retirement. Habitat for Humanity is a great
place to give away large items you are hanging
on to from your parents who died twelve years
ago. Whether for sentimental reason or just
never got around to it, it is finally time to get
rid of the unneeded useless items and start to
budget for new things and pay more things with
only cash. Offer 20 percent less to credit card
companies for a large credit card balance. If you
pay a lump sum, even 20 percent less, they will
usually accept that. The savings in interest you
will pay to credit cards far outweigh the lump
sum left in account sitting in the 401k, CD, or
retirement IRA gaining interest.

When you retire with a long-term marriage partner, expect to have an adjustment period. This will shock you if you are not prepared. Think of your husband of many years who has depended on you as if he were a nine-year-old boy. Please understand I am not being disrespectful, judgmental, and intending to label all men this way, but I use this analogy because a woman who has dealt with a nine-year-old boy can certainly understand what I am asking them to do. If the shoe fits.

Here is what may happen on a typical day as you begin a new schedule for retirement. Now remember, the schedule pattern you begin will be the groundwork you lay for your upcoming years. You may be a daytime person with lots of interests, and your husband may not be into football or baseball or any sports. He may have a hobby or two that he actively participates in but mostly enjoys hanging out, puttering during the day, and watching TV in the evenings. This is completely normal for newly retired men. Your husband may have lived vicariously through your busy exciting life, and he may have difficulty trying to occupy his extra time. Do not allow *his* boredom during the day to rob you of doing what you would enjoy or feel needs to be done. After all, you are retired too. This would be equivalent to you asking him to join you in the evening to go out somewhere when he wants to stay home and watch television. There is no difference. His special time in the evening is as valuable as your time. You would never require him to accompany you to a social event during his favorite television series. This would require him to take a shower, figure out something to wear, and visit with other people he doesn't really want to be with. Encourage him to find or invent a project or something constructive to do during the day and respect your special time, allowing you to get something done. My personal "Bill of Rights" was written to explain this. Number 5, which reads *I have the right to acknowledge and accept my own value system as appropriate for me without being subjected to the judgment or values of others!* This means when you get up on a nice, sunny Saturday morning and want to wash your car because it looks awful and your husband wants to go to the local fair for the third time, you can politely and without guilt or defense suggest he call a friend or plan it another day to attend with you. Likewise it could be the opposite circumstance. Your husband wants to work on a project either personal hobby or a home project during the week. On the weekend you may want to just relax and read a book, but your husband may want to clean all weekend. Saturday morning you may want to have some coffee, read the newspaper in its entirety, and make a big breakfast. Don't allow your partner to judge you and do not judge them or show any disrespect to them. There will need to be some compromising and strategizing to accommodate each other's desires. Just like figuring out for our kids, who would pick up little Johnny from soccer or get Susie to the dentist. If your husband wants to go do something and you are not interested, encourage him to go, then plan a time to meet together later in the day. We are all wired differently, and the hardest part about growing old and living side by side in retirement with a partner is to accept this concept. It doesn't matter if it is a ten-year-old marriage or a thirty-year-old marriage, the same rules apply. Habits you develop now will decide your happiness. I have learned you have to compromise as much as possible, especially when it comes to day-to-day decisions like which movie to watch or where you'll go out to eat. Marriage is a one-team game, so getting your way doesn't mean you won. You are both on the same team. Don't get complacent, however! Unconditional love should be for children and pets. In romantic relationships, you have to earn it—and re-earn it! Isn't that a good thing? If everybody just did what was good for themselves and based everything on the attitude "*what's in it for me*," can you imagine how it would change our world? It would destroy our society. There is an acronym for this—WIFM (*W*hat's *I*n it *F*or *M*e). Imagine a surgeon who was off his shift and a terrible accident needed his expertise and skills and he declined because he wanted to go home and watch the Superbowl football game. Imagine a garbage truck driver who spilled some items from the neighborhood trashcan by accident and just left it lying in somebody's yard. Imagine a teacher who heads off to the ski slopes all day on the "teacher planning day" that is provided to them with pay, shirking the responsibility of planning. Rules and regulations for adults are put in place for a reason. Some people are not very good at telling themselves what to do. This is the reason many cannot be self-employed and need an employer to tell them what to do. When you are self-employed, you get up and tell yourself what to do with no need for anyone to give direction. A *person of excellence* has an internal rule of not living with a WIFM attitude. My mother would remind us kids to stop the *"what's in it for me"* attitude often when I was growing up. It is a selfish lonely attitude to live by. "Your reward comes later" was my mother's standard answer. She was speaking about the rewards you receive later that you don't know about yet for the extra effort you make for someone else. The sacrifice is sometimes to not want your own way or be happy only when you get your own way. When your partner tunes in to the station WIFM and lives with that attitude daily and you don't confront them about it, you are risking your marriage. It could possibly be the demise of your marriage. You have to really take care of your marriage and watch carefully during the early years of retirement adjustment.

At age 4—Success is not peeing in your pants.
At age 12—Success is having friends
At age 16—Success is having a driver's license.
At age 20—Success is having sex.
At age 35—Success is having money.
At age 50—Success is having money.
At age 60—Success is having sex.
At age 70—Success is having a driver's license.
At age 75—Success is having friends.
At age 80—Success is not peeing in your pants.

It will come back to you when you take the high road. Tell him how important he is to you and show him how important he is to you regularly. Notice the grass freshly cut. Pay attention to the effort he makes to start dinner when you are running late. Don't make him the center of your universe, however! Don't allow him to make you the center of his! Pouring the entirety of your life's expectations for happiness into the hands of one mere person is a disaster waiting to happen. It's too much pressure. There is a balance of respect for each other's values, time, and energy spent on something. He ultimately wants to please you, so use good strategy to convey what you want. I suggest about a week in advance tell your husband three or four things you'd like to do that weekend. Say, *"Hey, honey, can you pick out one of these things to do and set it up?"* Your job is to let him know what makes you happy and his job is to plan it and execute it. If he is not a planner, however, don't sabotage yourself by acting disappointed or indignant that he didn't plan anything. Believe me, if he wants it bad enough, he will plan it. Marriage is like a marathon. Once you sign up, you have to continually train in order to be a success and compete. Even though in marriage there isn't necessarily an ending point, you still must train. Training doesn't stop because you switch partners and marry someone else. You just train differently, sometimes starting from scratch.

The chapter on disorders will help with this adjustment to retirement life. The signs are things like wanting to play all the time. They will have very little concern about the household duties, bills to be paid, groceries, or meals to consider. They will want to watch TV or do things that they probably have dreamed about doing when they retire for many years. Men are tied to their self-worth by their career success, and now they no longer have a career. You may take it personally, and you will find yourself looking at divorce. Many times it erupts into huge issues if you are not prepared. But if you are prepared for their behavior and just treat them as if they were fifteen-year-olds (angry, pouty, body flop tendencies) or nine-year-olds (irresponsible, wanting to play all the time without regard to anyone's needs other than their own), it just makes it easier!. You can work with it if you understand it. After raising kids, we know how to not allow bad behavior and take charge. We would never spend energy arguing with a nine-year-old or a fifteen-year-old. Come up with ideas for places to go, interesting foods to prepare together, and other interests that you may have to take the lead on. Don't expect them to suddenly pitch in and help you with responsibilities because they are now home full-time retired. They may behave as if they were nine years old or fifteen years old. Think back to your kids. Did they offer to do anything? Especially dishes? You may have to encourage the behavior at first. Not nagging. That is like a dripping faucet, and you will soon find yourself alone. They can become masters at ignoring you. It may take a few years to adjust to this new life. Don't be surprised if they suddenly put on headphones and wear their iPod around all day ignoring you, trying to find their happiness. They are merely searching, trying to find another world besides this world at home that is somehow different from what they have dreamed about for years. Sometimes the grass looks less green when you are standing in the middle of it than it did when you looked at it from afar. That being said, you have been warned!

Menopause

Some symptoms to embrace with menopause. Funny the word *menopause* is separated as *men! Oh pause*. Maybe that is why more women become divorced and are single during *men oh pause*! Interesting, isn't it?

Six Steps to a Stronger Memory

1. Learn something.

    Stimulating the brain helps it develop a resilience that allows us to fight off diseases, Paul D. Nussbaum, PhD, says, who has worked on brain health programs. Card games, musical instruments, puzzles, tennis, dance, and so many thousands of things to learn new! The YMCA and other community centers offer lots of classes for very little cost.

2. Sleep.

    Getting fewer than six hours of sleep a night can raise the risk of stroke. Try different bedtimes and see what time your body really likes. Maybe a later bedtime and later sleep-in time would better fit your lifestyle or your body. Menopause can disrupt the normal patterns our bodies have had in the past. There are no rules. You are running your own race, remember? Sleep or sex? If you are married, you may know that dilemma. Your libido will change for sure, but the average encounter is twenty minutes, says Linda Young, PhD, a Washington-based therapist who specializes in helping women foster healthy relationships. Your resistance may be a reflection of your satisfaction with sex or fear of intimacy, performance anxiety, or anger about something else in the relationship. This will affect your sleep and your memory.

3. Eat right.

More than half your plate should be filled with green, leafy vegetables. Get plenty of fish, nuts, and olive oil. Avoid refined carbs. A 2009 Columbia University study found that this kind of diet may help ward off Alzheimer's disease. It also will keep belly fat from creeping up so easily during menopause.

4. Challenge yourself.

The number one memory complaint people have is that they're bad with names, says neurologist Majid Fotuhi, MD, PhD. His prescription: memorize three names a day. Say the name when you meet the person back to them and say it again once to yourself.

5. Walk with a friend.

Psychiatrist Gary Small, MD, calls this a triple threat against Alzheimer's. It gives you a cardiovascular workout, stress-relieving social interaction, and mentally stimulating conversation.

6. Meditate.

   A quick calm-me-down: Inhale for a count of seven, hold for a count of seven, exhale for a count of seven. Repeat several times. Take up walking or running. Gardening can be Zen time too!

7. Listen to music.

   Your favorite song lyrics to recall or relearn will work your brain. Singing it will even add a challenge, singing harmony parts even more of a mental challenge.

Six Myths about Fitness after Fifty

- MYTH: Stretching becomes more important as you age.

- FACT: Research shows that stretching does little to prevent injuries and may even do harm. In a review of studies in *Medicine & Science in Sports & Exercise*, researchers found that stretching a muscle for sixty seconds or more causes a decline in performance. A stretched muscle, when released, contracts and tightens, the opposite of what you want to do.

- MYTH: The best way to burn fat is to work out longer.

- FACT: Exercising more does not help you lose more weight. In fact, a new study finds that it's *the intensity* of the exercise that has the most impact. Running five miles burns more calories than walking five miles does. Why? High-intensity exercise boosts your metabolism, says author Paul Williams, PhD, Lawrence Berkeley National Laboratory.

- MYTH: Cardio matters more than weight training after fifty.

- FACT: Weight training is just as important as cardio, if not more so, as you age. "You lose muscle mass with age and menopause, which causes a loss of strength," says James Hagberg, PhD, professor of kinesiology at the University of Maryland. While a loss of strength might not be noticeable at fifty, by sixty it will start to affect your ability to exercise at all.

- MYTH: Doing crunches will get rid of your belly fat.

- FACT: Targeting a specific area of the body for fat reduction, called spot training, just doesn't work. When you exercise, you're burning up whatever glucose and fat that's supplied by the bloodstream, not the fat that's right there on your body. The best way to get rid of belly fat? Eat smart and exercise consistently and move more during the day.

- MYTH: You shouldn't exercise if you're sick.

- FACT: When it comes to exercise and illness, your neck is the dividing line. If your symptoms are at or above the neck—sore throat, nasal congestion, and watery eyes—a workout is fine (unless you have a fever, then take a few days off). If your symptoms are below the neck—chest congestion, hacking cough, stomach flu—it's better to rest for a few days.

- MYTH: You burn the most fat when working out hungry.

- FACT: Exercise on an empty stomach and your body will tap into the storage of fat for energy, right? Nope. A 2011 study in *Strength and Conditioning Journal* found that the body burns the same amount of fat whether the stomach is full or empty. "Exercising without eating is not good," Maryland nutritionist Sue James says. A small snack can help fuel muscles.

Our Hormones

Listen and have a gracious attitude. If we have been successful in our careers or have a great self-esteem, we unintentionally tend to make others around us insecure. We can actually cause animosity without realizing it. This is true if the spouse or an individual has a wounded ego and has grown up with criticism by their parents. Our success can make some feel powerless. It doesn't make sense that our solid, secure self-esteem can make someone else insecure, but for some this creates animosity, and they begin to look for flaws that can be pointed out. Retirement soon allows lots of time to challenge you and to trip you up so you don't look better. Your spouse may try to blame your hormones as an easy scapegoat which will infuriate you if there is evidence of some animosity or game playing on his part. Make sure you don't frequently talk over and interrupt those who may take longer to gather their thoughts. Look at them straight in their eyes and rephrase whatever they tell you so they know you heard what they have said. We can be so busy thinking about what we are going to say next that we don't really listen. Taking a sip of coffee or beverage will allow your spouse to know you are taking a pause in the discussion allowing them to speak with less fear of interruption. Our hormones can play a part in how we hear something that may not have been intended to be hurtful or cause friction. Our spouse or friends can touch our emotions quickly, and before we digest what was said, we blow it out of proportion and instantly are convinced it was intended the way we heard it. Likewise, we may speak in a tone that comes across differently than it was intended without being conscious of it. Interestingly enough, a spouse or individual who has lost a parent at a young age will derive a boosted ego when they find someone who *is* successful and independent and marries them.

We are fortunate that hormone studies have begun to come back as we age. The Associated Press-Chicago did the longest most comprehensive follow-up yet of women given hormone pills during landmark government research. They found that many health risks faded and some unexpected benefits emerged. Advice remains unchanged: use hormones only in the short term, if needed, to relieve hot flashes and other menopausal symptoms. In a follow-up involving more than 27,000 women, researchers analyzed thirteen years of data, including up to eight years of information on what happened after women stopped taking replacement hormones—estrogen alone or with progestin. Check into hormones and see if the benefits for quality of life outweigh the risks. The research was launched in the 1990s to examine some of those beliefs, and the new results confirm that hormones should not be used for disease prevention. Using hormone replacement is an individual decision made case by case based on family history and other factors. Do your research and find out what you need to know to run your own race before deciding on hormones during menopause. Don't decide because someone you know is taking them. If we tend to be told by our friends and family members that we are more impatient or chatter endlessly or our mood is inappropriate, then pay attention.

Women Need to Depend on No One and Practice Happiness

A quality life demands quality work and quality leisure. But above all, it demands us giving ourselves permission to live fuller, deeper, and more daring lives.

Whatever You Practice Most, You Become!

If you are in the habit of being uptight whenever life isn't quite right, repeatedly reacting to criticism by defending yourself, insisting on being right, allowing your thinking to snowball in response to adversity, or acting like life is an emergency, then unfortunately, your life will be a reflection of this type of practice. You will be frustrated because, in a sense, you have practiced being frustrated!

When I practice a difficult drumbeat or a particular drum fill, it takes many hours and seat time, practicing it repetitively over and over. It would even keep me up at night many times going over it in my head while I am partially asleep. When I may try to push it out of my brain, it would go away temporarily and then come back. Our minds are powerful. This is why when you smile, your brain will light up. Tell yourself to smile, be calm, and relax. Eventually no matter how difficult that drumbeat may be for me, if I practice it enough, I will attain the goal and master the beat.

The same could be said for the drama queen. The drama queen has become so good at living in crisis mode that it is all they do. They practice this on a daily, hourly basis. This becomes such a habit because you keep practicing being uptight, allowing your thinking to snowball to every event in life. You keep practicing it; you'll be great at it. How about practicing how you want to be—composed during a crisis, deliberate with your decisions, controlling your thinking of negative outcomes. With practice you will master that instead. If this is you, stop. If this is your friend, tell her! She is wasting her life and losing friends as a result undoubtedly. Nobody is good at resisting their drama queen infection. You cannot inoculate yourself from their disease of drama. If you point it out to them, hopefully they will make a concerted effort to practice being happy and grateful on an hourly, daily basis. Just be wary of their disease so you don't become infected by them. Instead set an example of you controlling your life and your thoughts, not your life circumstances controlling you.

A Word about Social Grace

Have you ever watched birds eating from a feeder? You can always see there is one bird who is a bully. I have observed my feeder located on my back porch while sitting in the Jacuzzi many mornings. It is interesting to see that although there are four separate spots for them to all eat from at the same time, they consistently try to force another off and fight over one spot. If you watch long enough, you will see, there is just one that will peck at another bird, forcing it to leave and then not even utilize that spot he just chased the bird from, but sits guarding it from above. This one bird will spend time eating and moving about the feeder, pecking and bullying all the others. It appears that the other birds are toying and teasing this bully bird as they work to attempt to sneak a sitting on the perch to eat. You have to wonder why this one bird will monopolize this feeder as his very own. The other birds must deal with this bully bird and try to work around it. Nature is afflicted with the concept of "survival of the fittest." We, as humans, don't regard survival of the fittest as a social model for our behavior. So often we begin to act like birds or maybe someone you know begins to behave this way.

The brain of a bird is quite small, and it occurred to me that this bird has no social grace because it *has* a very small brain and instinctively has a strong survivor mentality or a WIFM (what's in it for me) mentality. If we pay attention to others around us, we can see this same bird pattern and behavior. Think about your family members or friends or coworkers you are around on a regular basis. There may be someone who everybody avoids or who monopolizes the conversation or the space in a room and thinks nothing about it. I have observed many people by their body language or mannerisms and how they speak. The way they speak gives an indication of the level of social grace they possess.

Birds are not taught this skill, but as humans, each of us individually should pay attention and learn the queues and make the effort to develop social grace.

It is time for us to look around at others in our lives, as well as ourselves and see if we are not getting along with someone on purpose. We waste an enormous amount of energy trying to be *right* or trying to *justify* our opinions or our decisions. It shouldn't matter! If you are running your own race, you don't need approval or to prove or support any thought, opinion, or decision.

Nothing in your life should ever be based on what someone else thinks, but merely what you think. This is not to the extreme of large purchases as a married couple. Obvious you would discuss a large purchase out of respect. But giving yourself permission to be *heard* is important. Give yourself freedom to enjoy your life and your retirement. This goes along with freely and fearlessly stating your opinion using social grace, of course. Making any decision with neither judgment nor bullying from anyone who would attempt to persuade your actions is true freedom.

If you are around a "bully bird" who is just being *mean*, don't cave in, just work around it. We are not birds with little brains, so acting as such by being controlling, bullying, or manipulative can make others uncomfortable. Lacking social grace will result in a bad reputation, which means we are creating that reputation unknowingly or maybe intentionally. Your brain has become very strategic by fifty years old, so someone lacking social grace or refusing to practice social grace could be creating a reputation to protect themselves on purpose. There are many mental disorders linked to this behavior. If you strike first and act like a bully, it will instantly push others away for a minute, putting distance or a wall of protection up. Practicing this "attack first" behavior only makes you better at it. It soon becomes part of your personality and essentially become who you are. In time you will be very lonely, as no one likes a bully.

Run your own race with social grace! Understanding this concept makes it easy to shrug your shoulders and think, *Well, they lack social grace!* "Letting it go and realizing that some individuals just don't care enough to take the time to learn social grace. Recognize that the person who is acting with no social grace is just like a bird that is pecking away at others, alienating itself and spending an enormous amount of energy trying to be the boss! Social grace is learned, some will never make an effort. Gracefully work around them and do what you want regardless. Listen to the song by Sara Bareilles, "King of Anything." It speaks of this very thing. Think what you want regardless of a bully bird's approval. *Run your own race!*

*Keep drinking coffee, stare me down across the table
while I look outside
So many things I'd say if only I were able*

*But I just keep quiet and count the cars that pass by
You've got opinions, man
we're all entitled to 'em
but I never asked*

*So let me thank you for your time
and try not to waste any more of mine
Get out of here fast*

*I hate to break it to you babe
But I'm not drowning
There's no one here to save*

Who cares if you disagree? You are not me
who made you king of anything?
So, you dare tell me who to be
who died and made you king of anything?

You sound so innocent
all full of good intent
swear you know best

But you expect me to
jump up onboard with you
ride off into your delusional sunset

I'm not the one who's lost
with no direction, oh
but you'll never see

You're so busy making maps
with my name on it in all caps
you've got the talking down
just not the listening

All my life I've tried
to make everybody happy while I just hurt and hide
waiting for someone to tell me it's my turn
to decide

Who cares if you disagree? You are not me who made you
king of anything?

Grateful and Ambitious

The happiest children and adolescent children are those taught two important principles that everything in their future will stem from: being grateful and being ambitious. This is something I firmly believe are the stepping-stone characteristics by which to base all the future characteristics.

When you are grateful, others want to do more for you. When you are grateful, you will take a low-paying job because you are not too good for it. Later as an adult, you are efficient at using money wisely and taking care of things because you are grateful for what you *do* have.

When you are ambitious, you are someone that others look up to and respect. As adults, it will obviously play a huge factor on the drive to work hard, go the extra mile, most likely be more active, which means healthier and ultimately practicing happiness. Tell your children who are raising kids (your grandkids) the importance of being grateful and ambitious in all aspects of their lives. This is the core of where all the other attributes such as being kind, self-sufficient, responsible, and ultimately being happy come from. Aren't those the attributes that we all want to see in our kids and grandkids?

Being grateful should be an everyday occurrence as adults. Live "favor minded" as Joel Osteen would remind us, and be grateful when it happens. That means when something good happens, like traffic going your way when you are in a hurry, your loan going through when it didn't look good, or you get an extra special something from someone without asking, say "thank you" and be grateful. Many times I have been out shopping, and for no reason at all, I would get special favors. Recently, I was at a store and the checkout lady asked if I would like to get a discount for Facebook Friday? I said, "Sure." She asked if I had a smartphone, and I told her I did. She said, "Hold up your phone and now I can give you your discount." Instead of using the coupon for 30 percent off one item I intended to use with my purchase, I received 25 percent off every item I was purchasing. Now I say to myself silently deep inside, "*Thank you, Lord, you are so good to me.*" I am grateful. Now I could easily attribute it to the fact that I was dressed nice that day and had perfect makeup, a smile, and a happy disposition, but I don't attribute those extra breaks to anything but God taking care of his child. It is being in a natural, continuous state of gratefulness that you walk around with, not of pride, like you are all that, but you are watching for all the things that go your way in life—a parking spot that opened up, the right person goes to the same event as you are attending and you meet someone who later becomes a business partner. You automatically realize it is in the plan of good events. In the Bible it clearly states "Goodness and Mercy shall follow you all the days of your life." You need to be consciously grateful and say thank you out loud if appropriate and to yourself under your breath, giving credit to God. Every time you do that, God will want to do more for you. Even as a natural father wants his kids to be happy and satisfied and have an easy life, so does God want that for all the world, but we have to accept it and say thank you. It's not a magic or voodoo thing. It is a demeanor of gratefulness that you carry, and it filters into the rest of your life, and before you know it, all you see in life are good things. You're so busy watching for the good and positive, you hardly notice the hassles and hurdles in life. Give it a try. Be ambitious when you get opportunities that are extra breaks and seize the moment and then be grateful for what it brings by verbalizing and acknowledging it. You must throw the seed out first before anything will grow. Ambitious in whatever venture or activity you are involved in will bring about some kind of reward. No seed for sure grows nothing!

I require the clients I see at the counseling center to start a journal, only writing good things that happen. Describing only the good things, not letting negative "woe is me" get any detail or time. Do this for a year and you will be shocked how much good you forget when you go back and read it!

The following is a letter written by an anonymous friar in a monastery in Nebraska late in his life. We need to read it and allow it to seep down into our tired and serious bones.

If I had my life to live over again, I'd try to make more mistakes next time. I would relax, I would limber up, and I would be sillier than I have been this trip. I know of very few things I would take seriously. I would take more trips. I would be crazier. I would climb more mountains, swim more rivers, and watch more sunsets. I would do more walking and looking. I would eat more ice cream and less beans. I would have more actual troubles and fewer imaginary ones. You see, I'm one of those people who live life prophylactically and sensibly hour after hour, day after day. Oh, I've had my moments, and if I had to do it over again, I'd have more of them. In fact, I'd try to have nothing else, just moments, one after another, instead of living so many years ahead each day. I've been one of those people who never go anywhere without a thermometer, a hot water bottle, a gargle, a raincoat, aspirin, and a parachute. If I had to do it over again, I would go places, do things, and travel lighter than I have. If I had my life to live over, I would start barefooted earlier in the spring and stay that way later in the fall. I would play hooky more. I wouldn't make such good grades, except by accident. I would ride on more merry-go-rounds. I'd pick more daisies.

Breaking the spell of rigidness and fear of the unknown requires risk and abandonment. Some view leisure as a right rather than a gift, but others view it as frivolous, unnecessary, and wasteful.

It's called the elder-brother syndrome—the compulsively responsible, upright, and uptight citizen. This person is one of restraint, denial, seriousness, almost martial control, frugality of everything, including emotions. This is technically called the *bionic individual.* The bionic person is described as, at least in appearance, above reproach. She or he works hard daily, each of her/his answers are quick and precise, and their time is managed with calculated economy. Above all else, no time should be wasted on such frivolous things as laughter and play when there is so much to be done in the world. Heavily laden with guilt and tension about each of the minutes she or he might be wasting! The bionic individual is stiff, fussy, meticulous, and many times incurably religious.

The bionic person simply does not have time to be happy. Irony of ironies, their commitment to this behavior has become a prison rather than a blessing. Being ambitious doesn't mean you can't enjoy the ride along the way. Even the Bible speaks of festivity, and Jesus was the prime host and the most popular guest of the parties and festivities. Jesus even was doused with perfume and attended to wedding wine and wedding garments. The Bible is full of merriment! The feasts by far outnumber the fasting.

Can we learn how to relax, play, and even celebrate in the midst of today's obvious chaos? How can we, with the pain we view on the evening news each night? Too often we get myopic and selective in our reading and seeking information only to affirm or justify our preconceived notions. Because we feel guilty, we apply the work ethic to our leisure experiences (lest we be thought of as lazy). Two of the symptoms of this attitude is we frequently become (1) overanxious and (2) exaggerate our own responsibilities. The need to romance our problems for attention can become such a habit that soon it becomes part of who we are. If we are always discussing how much we have to do, or how hard our life is, then we are practicing and perfecting this behavior.

The first step is letting go of the attitudes in the effort to being responsible *and* happy. Let go of the warm, comfortable, colorless, tasteless, abstract images you have of leisure and leap out of some of your routines or rut. Begin to refresh yourself in simple joys. Turn off your TV for a while and experience again the thrill of living your life directly rather than vicariously, without all the baggage and parachutes. Try a physical activity like bowling, ice skating, tennis, skiing, or dancing. If you always have the radio on, turn it off for an hour every day. If you always are in silence, turn the radio on for an hour.

What does it mean to relax? Despite hearing this term thousands of times during the course of our lives, very few people have deeply considered what it's about. When you ask someone what it means to relax, most will answer in a way that suggest that relaxing is something you plan to do later—you do it on vacation, in a hammock, when you retire, or when you get everything done. This implies that the other 95 percent of our lives should be spent nervous, agitated, rushed, and frenzied. This is an obvious implication that is in our subconscious minds. Could this explain why so many of us operate as if life were one great big emergency? Most of us postpone relaxation until our "in basket" is empty. Of course it never is. Relaxed people can still be super-achievers and ambitious. In fact, relaxation and creativity go hand in hand.

When I'm uptight, my drum playing shows it in every way. I can't be creative and feel the music if I am uptight. I tense up and tend to hit the rim of the drums and have less control of my sticks. When I am relaxed, it flows easily and quickly, and I can get around all the drum toms and be more fluid with my relaxed movements. Being relaxed involves training yourself to respond differently. Responding differently to the dramas of life is a conscious effort as well. It's called turning your "melodrama" into a "mellow drama." It comes, in part, from reminding yourself over and over that you have a choice on how to respond to life and circumstances. You will learn to relate your thinking as well as your circumstances in new ways. With practice (twenty-one days to create a habit), making these choices will translate into a more relaxed mental state even during a crisis. You can then be grateful after the crisis has been averted and recognize how well it turned out and how much worse it could have been.

Sadly, many of us continually postpone our happiness. It's not that we consciously set out to do so, but we keep convincing ourselves, "Someday I'll be happy." We tell ourselves we'll be happy when our bills are paid, when we get out of school, get our first job, a promotion. We convince ourselves that life will be better after we get married, have a baby, then another. Then we are frustrated that the kids aren't old enough—we'll be more content when they are. After that, we're frustrated that we have teenagers to deal with. We will certainly be happy when they are out of that stage. We tell ourselves that our life will be complete when our spouse gets their act together, when we get a nicer car, are able to go on a nice vacation, when we retire. And on and on and on! Meanwhile, life keeps moving forward. The truth is there's no better time to be happy and relaxed than right now, as you are living your life day to day. If not now, when?

Some people spend their whole life indefinitely preparing to live! Your life will always be filled with challenges. It's best to admit this to yourself and decide to be happy anyway. These obstacles *are* your life. Be happy anyway. Where you are now may not be where you will stay or be in the future. Get out of the rut and act grateful and ambitious!

Grief That Won't Heal

Mourning for most people no matter how intense follows a similar course. The grieving is all-consuming at first. Then slowly people begin to move on. But sometimes for reasons that scientists are just starting to unravel, the grief lingers and even intensifies. Until recently, unresolved mourning had no name or formal psychiatric diagnosis. It was often simply considered depression. Now mental health professionals identify it as a condition called *complicated grief.* Approximately

10 percent experience complicated grief. Why some people experience complicated grief and others do not is unclear. Women are more susceptible than men, as are those whose loved ones die suddenly or by suicide. Parents who lose a child are at especially high risk. Sometimes multiple losses within a short period of time can overwhelm someone. Katherine Shear, MD, director of the Center for Complicated Grief at Columbia University School of Social Work in New York City says complicated grief is often accompanied by an inability to face the finality of the loved one's death, as well as obsessive "magical thinking" about what might have been. Complicated grief was just recognized in this year's update of the *DSM* manual of mental conditions. If you feel you are dealing with this and it is interfering with your ability to find happiness, you will be unable to practice being happy when you cannot get through this affliction first. Counseling can be effective to those who need to get past a loss and begin moving forward.

Women need to rely on themselves fearlessly. You must believe that you will be okay by making good decisions, having a positive attitude, and responding to life as it happens with a calm, intuitive mind frame—looking only to yourself for decisions and answers that you research. Rely on no one to rescue you.

Women Don't Grasp Their Power and Importance

Women don't grasp their importance to the lives of their husbands, children, and all their relationships. This final chapter is very important. If you would like to accomplish something, you must first expect it of yourself.

Learn to embrace where you are. Be happy just where you are. Your feelings create the destiny of your life. *Run your own race!* What kind of attention are you placing on yourself? Who we are, what we have, what we do, what others think of us? Your subconscious mind responds to what you place into it. It is that simple.

You See It When You Believe it, Not You Believe It When You See It

Your subconscious mind is objective and unbiased. You need to be subjective and trust yourself that your future dreams are the present fact.

A Story

There was an executive who was interviewing for a new job. If he were to get this job, he would be leaving a job he had been doing for thirty years. This new possible job was a better executive position. He was so disappointed when he didn't get the job position. He found out later that the company he was applying for filed bankruptcy and closed. If he had been hired for that job, he would have lost all his retirement from his job of thirty years, and still not have a job.

Things are not always in our control and what seems like it is not in our favor may be exactly what would be to our best advantage.

A Story

There was a South African man who lived in a small city, and he was flying back to the United States. He had a friend who was picking him up and taking him to the airport. The friend called that morning and said he had car trouble. The South African man missed his flight and went back to his hotel after missing the flight and turned on the news. That flight he would have been on had crashed into a mountainside.

You will have many opportunities that don't work out the way you may have liked. You may never know how it would have affected you. Run your own race.

Life is a big racetrack that goes in many directions. You are the driver, and you can decide how fast to go, how slow to go, which turn to make. Each choice will be a domino effect, but you won't always have the assurance of the outcome. But if you use your intuition and your decision making skills, you will have a better chance to make fewer adjustments and remain happier along the drive through life. Ladies, you really are in the driver's seat. Speak up if your gut tells you something isn't right or doesn't feel right, even if it is met with roadblocks or discouragement and argument from others close to you.

Society baits us to the edge of disaster and then mocks us when we step over! Don't be a victim of society by following it off the cliff. You are in charge of your own life and your own happiness, which affects your spouses, children, and everyone in your circle of relationships. You set the standard, and others are watching you and will react accordingly. Many of us spend too much time practicing being unhappy, mostly because we worry about what others think of us secretly. We need to give ourselves permission to enjoy life.

Most of all we need to *practice* being happy. People have a tendency to cherish their dreams but rarely act to make them happen. Live now, not just look to the future with anticipation for happiness.

Put Off Procrastination

The habit of always putting off an experience until you can afford it, or until the time is right, or until you know how to do it is one of the greatest burglars of joy. Be deliberate, but once you've made up your mind, jump in. Maximum use of discretionary time *demands* creativity, planning, and good decision making. There is no such thing as lack of time. There is more than enough time to do what you *want* to do if you realize that you are the master of your time, *not its slave!* Control starts with planning. Two keys to remember:

1. Knowing what you want to do

2. Planning how to do it

Have you ever stopped to make a list of your goals and priorities for your leisure time? Boredom is one of the major causes of suicide and drug abuse in our country, and yet, we are shocked at the thought of throwing away life all at once *by suicide* and think nothing of throwing it away by parcels and piecemeal with our wasted time or lack of efforts or ambition. A very smart businessman, Jim Henderson Sr.—whom I have known many years and I admired for his diligence, efficient time use, and performance outcome in return for his efforts—told me to remember the six Ps, which means proper planning prevents piss-poor performance! Simple?

Addictive personalities are very common among our society now and plays a big part in procrastination, and here is why. Addictive personalities are people who go from one pleasure to another to another to another. This person could be your husband or someone you know. They cannot look beyond themselves. It is virtually impossible. It is simply who they are. They get up in the morning and have their coffee, they get something to eat, then they get in the hot tub or shower and rush off to work. Then they may come home, have a beer or glass of wine, maybe smoke some pot. They may go play with a hobby or stop off at a friend's or a local tavern ignoring anything else except when they will get their next fix and what it will be—when the next football game is on, when the next baseball game is on, what's for dinner, what's for dessert. They fixate on all the pleasures one right after another. They cannot say no to themselves. They are diseased with WIFM syndrome. Sex is usually an added addiction of pleasure after exhausting all the others (as long as you are willing). Don't let this infect you. Move on and ignore their behavior and procrastination. If something needs to be done and they haven't found time after spending so much time fulfilling their addictions, it's time for you to hire it to get done (they hate that). The most common comment would be "I was going to do that." But state your opinion or need and ignore any excuses. If you can do it yourself and it is not to their satisfaction, you may need to remind them of the three or four months that it was not completed. Allowing their pleasure-based lifestyle is destructive. It is a huge challenge you must contend with. This type of personality, the addictive personality, is very easily handled, but allowing it to not interfere with the normal flow of life and the responsibilities is difficult. My mother always had a favorite saying. It was "find something constructive to do." Make a plan and execute it. Don't let procrastination and deferring responsibilities to continue. Are you waiting for the addictive personality to come through?

Get Out of Your Ruts

Ruts are a form of *fear*. I believe in routine, but not in ruts. Dare to move out of some of the attitudes that enslave you. One of the biggest ruts for many is television—holding millions prisoner each year. Smartphones is running a close second. It has put more chains on more lifestyles than we could ever imagine. Few have the willpower to turn it off. But women hold the power to encourage a different behavior if done carefully and with a smile. Create a file, notebook, or bulletin board that stimulates both interest and order. Make it a priority to cut out games, ideas, places to go, things to do, notes, jokes, ads from newspaper or Internet sites to explore. Break out of the rut and your family and spouse and friends will follow you, remember (twenty-one days of doing it to make a habit).

Respect Your Time

Make laughter a priority. "A cheerful heart is a good medicine, but a downcast spirit dries up the bones" (Proverbs17:22). When your bones are dried up, you are dead. You can choose to be jubilant; likewise you can choose to be gloomy. Laughter will light up the brain and release chemicals that are extremely powerful as we discussed earlier in this book. "Dead" people are boring, and the people who are gloomy and have a downcast spirit are not good for you, and frankly, not much fun.

Schedule family time or couple time or friend time and go for it. Let life happen. Balance is a delicate art, but you should be convinced by now of the importance of balance. Great effort must be taken to seizing each day using rigorous discipline, which is necessary for quality leisure, laughter, and living in the present moment.

What are the most important things in your life? Our Society today pushes us to believe that the three most important things should be: money, possessions, and intimacy/sex. Not necessarily in that order. If you don't have money or lots of cool possessions, that only leave the last easily attainable important society-driven need, which is intimacy and sex. When all of our thoughts and decision making have these three as the determining factor in our lives and what we do, we are fools. Read 1 Timothy 6:9–10, which speaks directly about money.

Take away our money. Let's pretend we are homeless. Are we kind? Stingy? Critical of others? Suppose we have no fancy car, live in an old rundown home, wearing out-of-style clothes, who are we now? Are we still a happy individual? Are we content? Nothing should rule us. We need to freely decide to *create* the mood of the day, rather than let the circumstances and conditions of the day rule us and our life.

Take the gift of time and use it to the best advantage every day! Deciding to be happy regardless of money, possessions, or intimacy is real happiness. Someone will always have more money, more possessions and a more loving relationship than you. Value your time and make what you have, the best it can by utilizing every minute of your day in a balanced and productive way.

Analogy

Every morning the bank calls you and informs you that your account will be credited in the amount of $86,400 pennies ($864), but with the stipulation that it had to be spent that very day. No balance could be carried over to the next day. Every evening whatever sum you failed to use will be canceled. Think about what you could do with such a gift. You would probably draw out and use every cent every day.

We must treat our lives in this manner, utilizing and respecting our time, being cautious to plan strategically how we spend our lives. This includes driving our cars efficiently by planning our trips for errands that are in the same location or area. This includes picking up the house as you go along putting things away, compiling things to go upstairs together and bringing them up to put away one time instead of five separate trips. Consolidating your efforts for greater productivity gives you more time to do other things. We will then be respected leaders of our families and our relationships as they witness our efforts to utilize our time wisely. If we aren't constructively *contributing* to our relationships, we are destructively *contaminating* our relationships.

A study recently was done and published in the *Los Angeles Times* about boredom. There are five distinctive types of boredom. *Apathetic boredom* was quite common among high school students according to the study published in the journal *Motivation and Emotion*. Boredom isn't just boring; it can be dangerous to either the person who is bored or the people around them. People who are bored are more likely to smoke, drink, or use drugs. Kids who are bored are more likely to drop out of school and become juvenile delinquents. Studies also have linked boredom with stress and other health problems. Here are the other four types of boredom.

- *Indifferent boredom*, a relaxing and slightly positive type of boredom that reflected a general indifference to and withdrawal from the external world. Many retired folks suffer from this after ending their careers. Essentially they are checked out.

- *Calibrating boredom*, the slightly unpleasant state of having wandering thoughts and "a general openness to behaviors aimed at changing the situation."

- *Searching boredom*, the kind that makes you feel restless and leaves you "actively seeking out specific ways to minimizing feelings of boredom." This is also very common among retiring individuals who have few hobbies or passions.

- *Reactant boredom*, which is so bad that it prompts sufferers "to leave the boredom-inducing situation and avoid those responsible for this situation" (i.e., teachers). The big surprise in the data was the emergence of the fifth type of boredom.

- *Apathetic boredom*, which accounts for 10 percent of all boredom among college students and 36 percent of all boredom among the high school students. Thomas Goetz, a professor of empirical educational research at the University of Konstanz in Germany, and his colleagues recruited two sets of test subjects— sixty-three college students and eighty high school students. This revealed that students are indeed more bored than most. Boredom is not lazy. It is lack of mental discipline, which must be exercised. Finding a passion that makes you happy will quickly eliminate the boredom, and after twenty-one days of enjoying this new passion, it will become a habit. You will not have time to be bored any longer.

Don't fall into the trap of focusing on your every ache and pain and occupy your time by consuming your day going to doctor appointments. You soon can become obsessed with utilizing doctor appointments to keep from becoming bored. This is just a crutch to occupy your time and should not be considered a hobby. You will expose yourself to lots of sick people while sitting at doctor appointments every week, touching germ-infested magazines and chairs and doorknobs, even in the cleanest medical offices. Counseling my clients I see some who are older who have conditioned themselves to their main event of the week being a doctor appointment. This boredom, which is satisfied by doctor appointments, merely reinforces negative thinking, which leads to longer periods of depression.

Let's Understand Men for a Minute

Lots of people including men in our lives don't get it! Often men will measure success very narrowly, usually from a huge financial perspective. Men take pride in protection and providing for the family and bear private shame when they feel they have failed. They forget or ignore that we need love, support, interest, and caring. The caveman mentality makes them selfish. Allowing men to have the caveman mentality makes us selfish. Men really do want *Betty Crocker* in the kitchen and a *sex kitten* in the bedroom. And want it all after you get home from work and all without any expense. Men's egos are fragile. They do the "turtle routine"— shut down, pull inside, and aim their frustrations at you. Men act tough but hide their emotions. Their tears may be silent, but they run down the inside rather than the outside of their cheeks. They often control by intimidation to hide fear and doubt. They criticize and belittle to disguise a wounded ego. Bottom line, men want women to see through the macho mask. Women can make a huge, huge difference in the quality and course of the relationship if they understand these natural and society-driven tendencies. Women need the class and restraint to let things go at times, and not permit bad behavior at other times. Women must understand that men have been cornered into a small area of a living room essentially. If it were the cavemen days right now, women would be going out and killing the animal, bringing it home, gutting it, cooking it, cleaning the mess up afterward, and feeding it to everybody! We literally have taken away so much of a man's instinct to hunt and provide for the family. Their egos—at least for many men who are living with independent, dominate, menopausal women—have all but collapsed! We don't need to do *everything*. We deserve to be happy but never at the expense of a man who genuinely is willing to do things but is simply not allowed without our ridicule or judgment. This causes the turtle effect, and can you blame them? Equal respect for everybody's happiness is much more effective, physiologically speaking. Happiness is a decision you make and act on accordingly.

One doctor explained it to a woman's group this way. He said, "Little boy and little girl babies are identical at first. At conception they're both little girls. But early on in the pregnancy the boys get a big bath of testosterone, and that changes them dramatically. In fact"—he smirked—"it destroys a part of their brain, the part that thinks and feels like little girls think and feel."

What the doctor was pointing out was the true physical differences in the brain of men and women. You can't get a horse to think like a tiger. I believe women are more disappointed in men than vice versa.

Women's minds are more attentive to detail, which is sometimes uncomfortable for men's minds. Women seem to be able to think of six different things at the same time. A woman can carry on a phone conversation while she chops carrots for the soup, fixes peanut-butter sandwiches for the kids, and motions them in to eat while she's letting in the paperboy and getting out the checkbook, writing him a check, wiping the kids' faces, and sending them off to play...all the time planning what to make for dinner. Even women who are CEOs or presidents of large corporations must do six things at once from their polished oak desks in their penthouse offices overlooking a city.

If a man is on the phone and his wife whispers loudly, "Tell John we'll bring back the lawn mower tomorrow." The man usually looks confused, shakes his head to indicate he doesn't understand, and continues talking. She repeats the message, even uses body language to demonstrate the lawn mower being pushed, mimicking it in the living room, and saying loudly, "We'll return it tomorrow," but he continues looking totally blank. Finally he says with some annoyance, "Just a minute, John," sets down the phone, and asks, "What is it?" Only then can he comprehend the message. I know that is not true of every man, and it is unfair to generalize. I personally know men who can run circles around women when it comes to carrying on six different thought processes at the same time. I play with amazing musicians who have to multitask on stage under pressure all the time. They must decide which synthesizer patch to use for which song and which solo, all while recalling lyrics and changing the song to a different key. Practice always makes perfect

Understanding that it is not their fault and they are trainable is the good news. Kids need to be taught how to dust furniture, how to wash dishes, how to do things the way we want them done. Employees in new jobs require training, and employers expect to teach. People of all ages take classes to learn skills they didn't previously have. So it goes with a relationship. We expect each other to think and act the same as we do, but that is impossible. All we need is the open-mindedness to *teach* each other what we'd like.

Men can make terrific playmates! Most men are eager to participate in anything that smacks of fun. We women don't take enough advantage of that. Men are always up for an adventure. They have so much "little boy" still inside them that they can help us women be more childlike if we let them. Usually we won't because we are so busy being sensible we don't have time to play. Women need to talk and want to straighten out all our problems. It's good that we are the driving force to keep communication going, but we should have fun as well.

There was a study that showed baby boys make noises most of the time when they're experimenting with talking. Meaningless noises. But baby girls try to say words and string together in sentences even before they can actually talk. My son would shoot with imaginary guns making the noises. He would break off a part of a cracker or snack he was eating and aim it at the trees and make shooting sounds as he tossed it. At the same age, a little girl would be lovingly holding her baby doll. Men and women are wired different!

It's hard to know exactly how much of our differences in attitude and behavior is innate and physiological and how much is unconsciously learned from role models we observed. That thin line that separates the two will always be fuzzy. Some of the differences will diminish as society gets better at equality.

One thing for sure people either enjoy life or they don't. Getting married doesn't alter that fact. Getting older doesn't either. Old, young, married or single we decide to make ourselves happy or unhappy. Ideally we would strive to complement each other, each having strengths the other lacks. If we recognize that men focus on one or two things until they finish, then turn their attention to one or two more things it allows some grace. The fact is they are often less fragmented than women and more goal oriented. Often their endurance level is far superior to women's. Men put a more concerted effort into one task, spending the major part of their energy on solving that one problem before attacking another.

He flat doesn't remember details. But he can be trained to, if he realizes the importance of it. Wives may need to talk about a month before their birthday little wishes, list hints verbally as well as posting on a calendar by the refrigerator. Talk about it often. Describe the perfect birthday. Tell him where you would like to eat out and if you want him to get a sitter. This does take some of the fun out of it, but you have to do the training now. In just a few years he'll know what to expect, and you won't be so disappointed." They ultimately truly want to please you most of the time. They are still "little boys" inside. Just as a little boy says "look, Mom" for approval, men need the same reassurance and approval. It seems from my experience that the older they get, the more regressive free spirited they become. Men seem to be more sensitive about things than when they were much younger.

We are so good at caretaking and nurturing that in acting out love, we become motherly to our husbands if we are not careful. Ladies, don't fall into this trap, which is easy for women to do to men without realizing it. It's one thing to fix a scrumptious dinner, but insisting that he eat the vegetables is overstepping an unwritten boundary. Women have an amazing ability to notice people's needs and wishes. A woman at the dinner table usually sees when someone is looking for the salt and provides it right away. But if your husband is wearing a jacket that is clearly too large for him and he insists that he loves the jacket, bite your tongue and smile. Men don't care about fashion. Men care about comfort and affordability period!

Men think more broadly, in global terms, dismissing the trivialities as unimportant; fashion being one of the unimportant items for most men. Why do we entertain the idea, then, that a couple can easily communicate with pleasure for any great length of time? Here is a humorous but common conversation a couple had going home from a dinner party.

She: Carolyn is the best cook in town. The way she heated the brie just ever so slightly and then topped it with a sauce that was sweet but with some horseradish to make it zingy! Wasn't that good?

He: Good food.

She: She does everything like that. She must have had a million classes in gourmet cooking. There was mint in the vegetables too. I noticed that their friends from Nevada were pretty miffed with each other, did you?

He: Who?

She: The couple from Nevada

He: Who were they?

She: They sat right across from us. She was wearing a turquoise cotton top and a white skirt and lots of Indian jewelry, and he had on a denim shirt and Levi's. Did you notice his watch? Indian made. It had the biggest obsidian stones I've ever seen.

He: Oh, the guy who used to be a marine?

She: I don't know what he *did*. I just could see that he and his wife were hostile. Did you notice how she never laughed at his jokes?

He: He was a marine. He was telling us about the war. Fascinating stuff.

She: But I wonder why they were so mad at each other. When everyone clinked glasses during the toast, they avoided each other's.

He: We talked politics. He's a strong republican.

She: He sure drinks a lot. He had three scotch and sodas before dinner, about five glasses of wine during dinner and two brandies after.

He: (silent)

She: Did you notice?

He: Notice what?

She: How much he drank, I thought he'd fall asleep at the table, he looked so snockered.

He: (long silence)

She: So, what else did you guys talk about?

He: Oh, I don't know…the World Series…Iran… the tax law changes.

Do you see how different the sexes perceive life and what is important?

Make Their Day With Our Words

Our words are so powerful, and what we think and verbalize can set the direction of whomever you are saying it to—the old saying, "If you can't say something nice, don't say anything at all." We can have such an impact on others just by *how* we say something and by looking for the good in people and complimenting them. You could make their day and not even know it!

Run your own race and don't compare your circumstances or envy anyone else's race. You don't race a car looking to the side, looking behind you, or you would crash in a split second. Run your own race looking straight ahead, keeping aware of what is around you, and what to dodge and go around. We cannot allow ourselves to watch others and be critical or envious of how they run their race. It is our job to focus on ourselves and not envy or judge others and want what someone else has.

There is a saying I love: "Don't envy the rewards you aren't willing to sacrifice for." Just as it is difficult for most people to walk in others' shoes or circumstances and really feel their pain, it is difficult to know what sacrifices were made that you are unaware of to achieve the reward. How dare we feel envy toward them about it! Refer to chapter 8 (DAMP) personality.

The truth is, life is never as perfect as we would like it to be. People don't act as we would like, and there will always be people who will disagree with you or do things differently. But if you live your life fighting this major principle of life, you will spend most of your life fighting battles.

"Choose your battles wisely" is a very popular phrase for parenting but is equally important in living a contented life. Life is full of opportunities. You can make a big deal out of something or let it go, realizing it doesn't matter. If you choose your battles carefully, you will be far more effective in winning those that are truly important. Certainly there are times when you will want or need to argue, confront, and even fight for something you believe in.

Many people however argue, confront, and fight about practically anything, turning their lives into a series of battles over relatively nothing. There is so much frustration living this type of life you begin to lose sight of what is truly relevant. The tiniest glitch or disagreement in your plans can be made into a big deal. If your goal (whether conscious or unconscious) is to have everything work out in your favor *all* the time, then this is a prescription for a life of unhappiness and frustration. Choose your words to make someone's day better by acknowledging others, noticing their efforts, giving them praise verbally. Suddenly you will notice less wrong with your life and more right with it. Your words are so powerful.

Your partner's driving skills may become an issue for some women when you both retire. Perhaps you have always had trouble with being nervous with the way your partner drives the car. It isn't that they are bad drivers. Men tend to just drive more aggressively, and many times like they are the only one on the road. The problem with this selfish mentality is other drivers tend to speed up when they see you put your blinker on because they are also driving like they are more important. I've watched cars jockey for position while merging into one lane and play chicken till the last minute, only to honk their horn because the car is now ahead of them by one car. So take deep breaths when your partner drives and compromise to allow fifty-fifty driving privileges for each of you, which can solve this dilemma. Sharing the driving privilege allows your partner to sit in the passenger seat occasionally and feel the helplessness and "out of control" feeling once in a while too. Everybody's driving style is different, but when you were both working, you didn't spend as much time driving together daily and traveling more, so this will possibly surprise you. You have been warned, watch out! Pick your battles, but if you truly have anxiety about close calls with other cars when your partner is driving, step up and say something. If you experience headaches after a trip in the car with your partner for no apparent reason and you have gasped in fear several times during the car ride, it is likely your cortisol level has spiked very high, causing symptoms. There is a problem so address it, or the anxiety will build and grow. Your words and how you say something can be carefully chosen and very kindly spoken to avoid accusations. Dwell on your anxiety, not his driving style. Your anxiety *is* real. Do not allow him to dismiss it as "all in your mind." Begin the fifty-fifty driving agreement and he will quickly understand how *real* it feels. I am not suggesting to drive recklessly and scare him. Trust me when I say he will find fault and even look for it while you drive. Your best defense…say nothing.

Men Don't Want to Be Alone, Just Left Alone

If you are under the delusion that your spouse will retire and finally get to the tasks that have been deferred for months or maybe years, you are very wrong. Yes, the excitement of not having to get up to go to work will spark a short episode of enthusiasm in him to get a particular project completed. But very quickly that will wane. There will be some boundaries and dilemmas to confront if you want to avoid some huge issues that can create explosions that are unnecessary.

He just wants to be left alone. Retirement is a transition. At least at first! Your newly retired spouse has to adjust, and he needs the grace to digest this change. If you have been a stay-at-home wife or have retired prior to your spouse, you already have a pattern or schedule established. This is where the problem can lie. Here are a few dilemmas to look at to establish an understanding, making this transition of a new lifestyle more comfortable and less explosive. How you act or react now can set up the future dynamics of your household and possibly your future retirement chemistry, which may be delicate.

- *Dilemma of sleep patterns*

    You may love to sleep late. Your body may require less or more sleep after the hustle and bustle of working pressures are removed. As you relax into your newfound freedom, pay very careful attention to your body requirements and how you feel with different sleep patterns. Accommodating your spouse by getting up at 7:00 a.m. could work for your spouse, but may turn disastrous for you. If you tend to stay awake until midnight or 1:00 a.m. or take longer to wind down, your body will be deprived of necessary sleep you require. This will ultimately cause you to gain weight, especially during menopause, as well as alter your mood and metabolism. You may need to examine what works for *you*. Too bad if he wants you to go to bed at ten thirty with him every night and wake up at 6:30 a.m. Too bad if you would like him to watch a movie at midnight or sleep until 8:30 a.m. Both are acceptable, but it is grueling to adapt to something your body is absolutely fighting. There is no normal. Normal is what works for you!

A personal example: I attend rehearsals for my bands on Tuesday evening from 5:30 p.m. till around 9:00 p.m. and Wednesday nights from 5:30 p.m. until around 9:00 p.m. I am still pretty alert by 9:30 p.m. when I arrive home. My husband has a routine that works well for him to be awake at 7:30 a.m. and likes to go to bed around 11:00 p.m. I arrive home after rehearsal, and I finally put my feet up and chill out after a busy day of counseling clients in the afternoon and rehearsal in the evening. We chat about our day and possibly watch a comedy together; then he goes to bed at 11:00 p.m. After he goes to bed, I can now read the paper if I was not able to do so in the morning or maybe sip on a beer before thinking about bedtime. In the mornings David will make coffee for himself and have my coffee ready when I awake at 8:30 or 9:00 a.m. If I wake up any earlier in the morning. I run out of steam by 8:00 p.m. while rehearsing on my drums. Wednesday evenings I occasionally spend an hour or more at the local pub after rehearsal visiting with a few of my girlfriends. This allows me girl time to talk and vent and laugh. Don't forget how important it is to laugh. It is healthy to laugh at situations. Another repercussion of *not* enough sleep is you will tend to not laugh at anything! When you don't get enough sleep, you remain lethargic and run out of gas quickly, which leaves you frustrated at yourself.

Try different patterns of sleep and wake-up times. Pay attention to how you feel, how your mood and appetite react. Your level of activity will also fluctuate to compensate for your lack of sleep.

Be careful that you don't sabotage yourself by trying to coordinate your sleep pattern to accommodate your partner's. This one element to your daily pattern can make your life easy or hard. Your intimacy will find a way to show up even with limiting your time in bed together, so you won't have to worry about that.

- *Dilemma of eating habits*

  Wow! Was this a huge eye opening dilemma? Yes, it was! I have always been conscientious about my food intake, but I had never paid attention to how different David's idea of food was. Although he knew the nutritional values of food, due to my influence and encouragement through the years, it did not become really important until his heart attack in November of 2011 at age sixty-two. Many factors were at the cause of his heart attack, but afterwards eating healthy became less of a battle. David began making an effort to eat healthier. He enjoyed eating leftovers for breakfast in the morning. We are not talking just pizza. I am much more traditional and enjoy breakfast foods! This was a meal that we soon created individually for ourselves in the morning. Creating separate breakfast food eliminated the problem of either of us feeling they must eat something out of pure obligation that has been prepared. Healthy foods that I enjoy is not always a favorite of David's. We made a rule that each of us would prepare whatever we were in the mood for in the morning for breakfast. This was an easy compromise.

There were more difficult compromises to acknowledge within a short time of our newly developing retirement lifestyle. David likes to eat dinner at 5:00 p.m. or 6:00 p.m. It is just his preference. My preference is to eat whenever I get around to finishing a job or a project or drum practice with no specific time. Since David did not usually eat lunch, he was quite hungry by 5:00 p.m. or 6:00 p.m. One solution that resolved this dilemma was having four o'clock happy hour during the Judge Judy television show. This allowed me time to cut up celery, crackers and cheese, or an assortment of nuts to take the edge off and allow for more time to wrap up my day before helping with dinner. This helped delay the urgency of dinner at exactly 5:00 p.m. or 6:00 p.m. and kept any blood sugar dips at bay. This would also keep from bad mood swings or confrontational demeanor, due to hunger from either of us.

Dinner time frames for each day as well as several menu items to choose from were discussed early in the day. This made it easy to be on the same wavelength. When defrosting a cut of meat from the freezer is necessary and one partner is out running an errand, the other has some idea of what is planned, so they can begin preparing.

Coffee in the afternoon was something I discovered very valuable. It took the edge off our appetite if we were out shopping and didn't want to eat fast food. Our best discussions and ideas were while drinking coffee and brainstorming about things. Our coffee time most days is three or four in the afternoon.

Variety is the key to keeping the spark in eating at home. Give each other a chance to try new and different dishes without judgment. Invite a couple over and try a new dish out. Now that you are retired, you may go out to dinner less often, so cut out recipes from magazines and try them out. Quick meals were convenient, but now are unnecessary. You may

RUN YOUR OWN RACE

still be very busy even now that you are retired. But you can enjoy the luxury of a little extra time to marinate some meat or make a special dish that takes more preparation time than you used to have.

Be creative. Sneaking a handful of fresh bag spinach in a soup or stew when your spouse isn't looking is not a crime. The spinach cooks down to nothing and you can't even see it or taste it, but the micro nutrient value would shock you! I put a can of black beans in my brownies in place of the oil and less sugar in any sweet desert recipe and its amazing nobody knows!

- *Dilemma of hobbies and activities*

This was probably the most difficult and stressful as well as disappointing element of retirement dilemmas. I am naturally a workaholic. I derive an unnatural amount of pleasure in getting something done or helping someone else get something done or accomplished. I would choose tackling cleaning out the garage, shed, closet, or yard work before I would choose to go do an activity for fun. When I was working, I was always working on at least three home projects at the same time, deriving a huge sense of pleasure. But I could never derive that same pleasure while doing something fun!

No company is better than *bad* company! This is probably the best advice I could possibly pass along to anyone who is retiring with a spouse who is profoundly different in activity level or interests. This means that you enjoy what you want without judgment or subliminal sabotaging from each other. Activities at home or on vacation should be fun for both you and your spouse. If they are not fun, then do the activity with someone who enjoys it the same. When I was busy working in real estate, this apathy to fun would occur, especially when doing a fun activity with my spouse. I surmised that it was because I was still thinking about work and not able to relax enough to really have fun. I was very concerned and baffled as to why I did not enjoy relaxing and doing things that should be fun. I thought, *After all, everybody else appeared to be having fun.* It did not become clear until after I retired. I realized I was not enjoying the activity or adventure because I didn't choose it! It wasn't until I started asserting myself as to what I thought would be fun to do and doing it that I realized it wasn't me, but merely the activity choice. Further exploring myself I discovered it was because it did not have the elements necessary for it to be fun for *me*. It was not rewarding enough for me. I would be happy to do something as long as it was tied in with something productive. An example of a fun event for me would be the beach cleanups. David and I belonged to a Jeep club when Nicholas was about five years old. We were involved in the beach cleanups because it merged driving the Jeep in the mud with a purpose of cleaning up the beaches. Thinking back I remember really enjoying this event.

I personally did not enjoy long drives. It was a favorite thing for David to do, but to me it was a big waste of gas! That was back when gas was ninety-nine cents a gallon too! Men you will notice that as they age they will want to go on long drives because that is what their parents used to do for relaxation and fun. Now it is just stressful to me unless you are in Montana or Utah where there is no traffic or idiot drivers. I also did not enjoy sitting and watching movies all day at home. That was a waste of too many hours unless I was polishing something, sewing something, or folding something.

Activities that David and I enjoyed for fun when I was young were merely repeated because I hadn't yet developed or chosen any of my own interests or fun activities.

Women tend to be unassertive and ignore what they may *want* or enjoy. They do this in order to adapt to who they are with. They may also do this to simply satisfying what is being required of them or avoid any confrontation and keep the peace. Now it is time to change that and grow a spine, ladies!

When I would visit a museum while vacationing for many years with David, I did not tend to linger very long. It was enjoyable and interesting, but I would not read every piece of literature available. I would have to drag David literally out of a historical museum or hurry him along. It was as if he wanted to make sure he was getting his money's worth. David loves to be knowledgeable about a variety of things. My short attention span would ruin the fun factor. I would find myself becoming edgy and bored. I just enjoyed things differently with less emphasis on memorizing facts and details. For me and many like me, it's only fun if it comes easily and effortlessly.

If you don't enjoy all the same things, take a vacation alone or with your girlfriends and have fun. Give your spouse an opportunity to take any type of vacation he wants without you as well. Together you can also plan a week each year somewhere you both enjoy without interruption. He may just want to sit and read. You may like to go kayaking or do some shopping.

Recognize and identify who your spouse is and what he enjoys if you don't already know. He may enjoy a vacation or a hobby differently. Each of you must consider the other and enjoy a vacation your own way for each of you without judgment.

When I was young and while raising our son, our yearly vacation was very important. It gave all of us a break away from work and home to enjoy time together. When our vacations were budgeted tightly, it was a challenge, but we enjoyed the simple things. Camping and driving was the usual ritual each year, whether it be to Idaho, Montana, California, or Oregon. We took the train across the United States to New Jersey when Nick was about ten years old as a family and a few cruises to Mexico as well.

The element that you may be missing could be variety. But make sure it includes elements of fun *you* enjoy, not forced out of obligation or a rut.

- *Dilemma of intimacy or lack of intimacy*

This will be a whole new paying field now that the work pressures are not present. I can assure you that men gauge the temperature of a relationship by how often you are interested in sex. Men don't understand that our libido is slowing down for some of us. It is different for each woman, and it shifts slightly every year. Men are expecting that retirement will allow them more intimacy since there will be more time. What may not be considered is that as a man ages, his testosterone levels change as well, and he will have to adapt to the unrealistic expectations he may have for himself as well as you.

A woman gauges a relationship temperature by intimacy *outside* the bedroom. A pat on the butt! A kind compliment, doing something that he knows you would like. It can be something as simple as filling up the bird feeder that he knows you maintain and keep full of seed. Making an effort to please you during the daytime. Other examples such as washing the car for you, tackling a chore that he has been procrastinating about completing also are essential and considered foreplay. You can never reward bad behavior with intimacy in the bedroom. If there is no intimacy outside the bedroom, you just can't get into the right frame of mind. For a woman, it starts outside the bedroom.

Date night can be established! I preferred to do a happy hour every day. This consists of being home around four o'clock each day during the week. If I am working on a project or playing drums, I stop and we meet together on the couch around 4:00 p.m. We can usually watch Judge Judy while discussing different events of our day during commercials. This allows us a *no pressure* connection time! The beverage of choice can be alcoholic, coffee, or a healthy blended smoothie. What you choose to drink is immaterial. My husband used to say a cute motto, "Candy is dandy, but liquor is quicker." If you set up an opportunity with good conversation, a tasty adult beverage, and you are both free from any underlying arguments or resentment early in the day, it is bound to become intimate. Dinnertime can be a setup for some action as well if you work together on a meal. TV time robs relationships of intimacy, but used strategically can be a form of connection if you both enjoy a particular show. We always eat at the dinner table and talk about our day. It would be easy while retired to sit and eat while watching the news or a television show, but I began the habit of dining at the table. There will be less to discuss because he is not working and you are not working. But your hobbies, friends, ideas, goals, and anything else you may have separate or in common with the topics now. Intimacy starts by looking directly into the eyes of your partner when they are speaking. Listening to their voice inflections and observing their body language. If you are not contributing to the relationship by making this effort, you are destructive to the relationship. Intimacy begins outside the bedroom.

Don't get caught up in what I call "obligatory sex." It will be relentless and unsatisfying, and it is a form of control. Some men only derive their sense of self-worth by intimacy with their spouse. They will continuously pressure you with little innuendos during the day or correlate conversations with a sexual undertone. It becomes very tiresome and causes indifference, which is the opposite of what he may be trying to achieve. Allowing some playful silliness can sometimes keep him feeling special without making it a drawn-out ordeal.

I have a close friend who has a rule that her retired husband shower every day. This is the biggest respect you can give your partner. Intimacy will be more desirable and more often if you are smelling good. If you are waiting several days *now* to shower as a standard, imagine when you are seventy-five years old how many days you will be pushing the need for a shower. Soaking in the Jacuzzi doesn't replace a shower or bath. Retirement makes it so easy to slack off on good habits like brushing your teeth, showering, or even getting out of your sweatpants in the morning, but make the effort. It takes twenty-one days to create a habit of not doing something or doing something.

- *Dilemma of chores*

Earlier we talked about using the strengths of your spouse to benefit your relationship and happiness. Now that you are both home it may be implied that you can finally be the little Susie homemaker and take care of all the household responsibilities. This may not have been your idea of how you imagined spending retirement. Talk about the chores of your everyday life. Divide them up into nonnegotiable chores and the negotiable chores. Priorities are different for every individual. The nonnegotiable chores are paying bills, emptying the recycle and garbage, cooking meals, grocery shopping, Christmas shopping—things that are absolutely necessary to your life and must be done each month. The dilemma lies in the category placement. What is absolutely a nonnegotiable chore with a specific frequency will be different for a woman than a man. A woman may need to clean the refrigerator out often because of storing lots of leftovers. A clean refrigerator may not matter to a man, but be very important to a woman.

What tends to happen is a woman will try to influence her spouse to see things her way and her sense of priority on chores. Compelling your spouse to make something just as important to them is futile. Forcefully convincing them that if they don't agree it means they don't really love you. It is unfair to expect others to buy into your insanity!

Make separate lists away from each other for all the negotiable and nonnegotiable chores. Then set a good time when you are relaxing together with maybe a bottle of wine and compare your lists. This will bring about enlightenment clarifying each other's expectations and levels of priority for chores. Using the knowledge of your spouse's priorities and expectations can be helpful. You can create a starting point to share the responsibilities and the chores now that he is home and retired and able to contribute.

An example situation of unrealistic expectations would be the priority I have to make sure that the hummingbird feeders are full and the bird seed feeders as well. I could be relaxing in the Jacuzzi hot tub outside in our backyard deck and look over at the bird feeder and notice it needed seed. I would literally get out of the hot tub and go get the bag of seed in the basement right then. This was a large twenty-five-pound bag too! I would fill up the feeder, all while in my bathing suit, and return back to the hot tub. David could wait a week with an empty bird feeder and not worry about filling up the feeder. It would be unrealistic of me, however, to expect him to notice it was empty or expect him to fill it. You are expecting him to buy into *your* insanity. I'm the one who cares about the birds.

- *Dilemma of money*

    Both of you may have worked to pool your income and retirement savings, but never forget money is extremely important to a man. A man's self-worth is tied directly to their jobs and the nest egg of money they have saved. It is not based on who contributed the most in dollar amount because that would be difficult to determine since many households have breaks for career changes, job losses, and children to stay home and care for.

    What is important to a man is to be on *his* team. Being on his team means stretching the dollar at the grocery store and paying attention to budgeting every area of your household. This requires looking at the auto insurance policies you currently have in force, making sure you are not paying too much by comparing it on a regular bases. Your homeowner's insurance, the interest rate on the primary home you are currently paying, the cable company and cell phone plan you are paying should be monitored regularly. Many times by a simple phone call, checking or comparing can save you hundreds of dollars per year.

Make sure you brag about your researching for the best rate, shopping for the best deal at the store, or anything else you do to help save *him* money. This means so much to a man! This is a powerful team effort. Men will not always pay attention to your efforts, so you must toot your own horn regularly.

Money is a very emotional thing. As a real estate agent I became very aware at how money can play havoc with a person's emotional stability. As we know, money is the root of all evil! People will fight over money after a death in the family, murder for money in order to not have to pay child support or support an ex-wife. It is easy to allow money to direct our decision making process, ultimately making it our god.

The power in any relationship typically shifts to the one who is bringing home the income. Retirement has evened the playing field when both you and your spouse are not working. Now *neither* of you is working. However, now you both will share in the spending of your nest egg for leisure, household repairs, and living expenses equally. Try to resist the temptation to criticize his desire to purchase something, even if you feel it is ridiculous or irresponsible. You will have more power in persuading him to rethink a purchase by being interested and supportive. Looking at all the pros and cons with him will provide the necessary information for a decision that is prudent. But watch him! When he is contemplating a purchase, if you pay close attention, you will see him work every angle to either talk himself out of spending the money or take an enormous amount of time researching it to get the biggest bang for the buck. Many times never purchasing it using an excuse that they justify. He doesn't want to spend any money. Practice being supportive without judgment and criticism and not trying to control every dollar that is spent. This will prove difficult at times. You both are deserving of using nest-egg money to enjoy your retirement as you choose. Your spouse will also need the same latitude to enjoy his retirement to the fullest. It can be more difficult for a man to spend money especially if he has always relied on you to do the spending at the grocery store or clothes shopping. He may have a stroke when he looks at how much it costs for things now. If he is actively participating in the spending now, you must be patient. Be ready to hear about it for days sometimes after a big purchase. Especially if the purchase doesn't directly benefit him in any fashion.

Consider making a short-term list and a long-term list for things you want to spend money on together. Keep in mind there will always be unexpected incidences such as vet bills for pets, car problems that are very expensive, or house repairs such as a roof, which can be thousands of unexpected dollars to pull from the nest egg you have saved.

Contact your financial advisor and have him do a data input calculation of how much money you will have remaining based on factors. This allows you to see what you have at age seventy-five and eighty-five years old and older. Your home may be paid off in fifteen years, which will allow for less to be needed to pull from your retirement for a mortgage payment. Other factors such as additional social security incomes bringing more money into the household requiring less drawing from your principal nest egg (i.e., IRAs). This information will direct you as to how much you can spend monthly now and later.

- *Dilemma of judgment*

Judgment starts to creep into your everyday schedule, and it can begin to create tension. Here is where you must say to yourself often, *This is how I want to enjoy my retirement.* It is also what you must repeat to yourself when you see your spouse spending a whole day doing something that seems ridiculous to you or a big waste of time in your opinion. You or your partner is not entitled to a *say* in each other's activity or projects regarding use of time.

An example would be when I am washing my makeup brushes individually with a bar of soap, cleaning each one and placing them on a towel. I am doing exactly what I want to do. It does not affect anyone else. I now am grateful I have the time to do such small tasks that while I was working I barely had time to do. My working life of every day getting up and going to work, no weekends off and feeling like I never had enough time for little tasks is in the past. As most women know, handling the shopping, cleaning, cooking, and keeping up with laundry for wardrobe selection was all-consuming while working. Now I can take the time to putter around with a sewing project, or work on a drum part if I feel like it or even watch TV and read the paper longer than usual in the morning without any underlying judgment or animosity.

Likewise I must refrain from judging my spouse for his indulgences or self-absorption—shooting his gun at the range or racing his RC car at the track a few days a week, or puttering in the garage for hours. I remind myself, *This is how he wants to enjoy retirement.* He is not affecting anyone else.

If I continually left a mess everywhere I went, then it would definitely create some tension. If I was cleaning my hairbrushes or makeup brushes in the bathroom sink and left a large brown makeup ring in the sink and didn't clean it afterward or left the brushes on the sink counter for four days, then it is absolutely affecting my spouse.

If your spouse began working on his motorcycle engine in the living room on the carpet and left all the pieces and parts to step around for a few weeks, this would be inconsiderate and would certainly be affecting you.

Constant consideration is the key to keeping judgment from creeping into the atmosphere. Once little inconsiderations begin, it soon will be a cat and mouse, tit for tat game, and will become vicious quickly!

Discuss this dilemma of judgment before retirement. When either is tempted to question why they are doing a particular task or project, hobby or vacation, remember the statement: *This is how I want to enjoy my retirement.* Regardless of the order of priority that may or may not be synchronized, they are who they are, and each of you can enjoy retirement as you wish.

Don't be afraid to express an area of inconsideration that highly affects you and makes you tempted to *be* judgmental. You are both living under the same roof all day long now, so be mindful of triggers and discuss any concerns immediately. Don't wait or build up animosity, which later is explosive.

An example, my husband is using model glue to repair his RC truck in the living room one evening while watching TV. This highly potent and stinky glue can be used when I am out of the house at a band rehearsal two nights a week; therefore postponing this project allows it not to affect me in any way.

Another example, the loud volume of the TV or radio. We all love to rock out to the music; after all I play in a loud band often. For years my husband would listen to everything really loud. Because his hearing loss is significant, he naturally listens to movies, the radio, and most things very loudly. Other friends or family members would visit and comment about the volume level. I had become accustomed to it over the years, but after retirement it became exhausting and bothersome on an everyday basis. When I was at work, I wouldn't be affected by it. I had a quiet office for eight or more hours a day. My husband had to create a habit of turning down the TV when someone was speaking or someone came into the room. This was a challenge, but attainable after making it a habit.

Another example, I talk on the cell phone loudly. I do this unconsciously. My husband does not want me talking on my cell phone in the kitchen where he is listening to the radio or watching TV trying to hear over my phone conversation. Ladies, men don't want to hear you on the phone talking to your friends. They don't care about all the drama! They may watch drama on TV, but they don't want to hear you on the phone around them. Go in another room or take your basket of laundry to fold in another room while chatting on the phone. Even better, if possible go have coffee with your friends.

Once you discover what you really like to do, you can move toward doing it with no judgment from anyone else. Run your own race and enjoy your retirement.

I have discovered how much I enjoy the quiet. I need quiet time to rest my brain more than I realized. Some may want the radio or TV on twenty-four hours a day for company. Each individual is different, and that is why judgment is so destructive to our growth and happiness. Fear of judgment from your spouse can ultimately rob you of your happiness. Say to yourself and state this out loud often, *This is how I want to enjoy my retirement!* Have this important conversation before retirement.

I have an analogy I created when I was sitting in my hot tub trying to figure out my relationship and marriage that was becoming completely out of control. It is what made me begin thinking I would write this book! It is what sparked my thought of how important this analogy would be along with using other analogy's in the book. This analogy was very helpful in my healing process during my road through a divorce that has still not yet happened and may or may not happen in the future.

Imagine a large elephant that represents life. You can *feed the elephant*, which is having fun and doing activities that you enjoy by yourself or with others. Things such as hobbies, carnivals with the kids or grandkids, all the fun stuff, being happy-go-lucky and not concerned about the next event or consequence in life or any responsibilities. Or you can *pick up the elephant poop*, which is correcting avoidable mistakes, doing the responsibilities regarding money, kids, and general living responsibilities, planning vacations, dental appointments, and being in general everything to everybody. Or in my case, everything to my husband. You continually go around and clean up the poop from behind the elephant, which is not fun. Necessary to do, but should not be done entirely by yourself.

The balance is doing both feeding and picking up the elephant poop 50 percent of the time equally. No one should be allowed to just *feed* the elephant and not have to clean up some of the poop at least some of the time. No one should have to just pick up the poop that never ends while someone is always feeding it. It should be shared fifty-fifty for a fair, balanced, and happy life. If you cannot get your spouse to help come around to the back of the elephant and help pick up the poop, you will soon be up to your knees in poop or worse drowning in it. If they are gleefully and thoughtlessly feeding the elephant without any regard for you and refuse to help you with the cleanup, run…fast…run your *own* race. They may feel that you caused your own poop, but that does not change the reality that it is still there! It is still up to your knees! Discuss the poop with your spouse, and if the consensus declares it as diarrhea and unnecessary, then *together* get it under control, but do it together. Everybody deserves to feed the elephant and not get stuck only picking up the poop.

Conclusion

This book was written while I was separated from my husband, whom I married at the age of twenty-four. Now at age fifty-five I have taken the time to regroup and understand myself better. It was written while I lived alone in our luxury condo, which we purchased along with seven other properties while I was in real estate. Over a course of a year while separated, I did an enormous amount of research on many subjects. Anybody who knows me understands how I can be overly ambitious and focused with a tendency to become consumed by a goal. My final wish and desire for the outcome and purpose for this book is to prepare others for retirement. To encourage others to always look up and listen to that quiet spirit deep down that you may want to ignore. Pay attention when you feel uncomfortable around someone. Slow down when you feel you should, don't make that purchase if you don't have a good feeling about it. It is the discernment that something is not right. Ask yourself if God sees the big picture, could you avoid a tragedy? We all cry out to God when we are in trouble—in a car accident, terribly in debt, sad from a loss of a loved one or impending loss of a job. We all naturally do that. Why? Maybe it is because secretly, deep down, we want to believe someone bigger up in heaven could care about our situation and somehow save us or at least help us. Even if you don't believe in God, should you be wrong, what risk could you be taking? There are no do-overs when you are dead. It's too late to believe in God by then. Wouldn't it be nice to have someone to talk to and feel heard? Fill your heart with a good spirit inside. Don't rely on other people for direction. God won't ever allow a major mistake in your life without some warning, but you must be intuitive and be listening. You must be listening and aware of your feelings. Run your own race because God is watching and listening and whispering. You can't hear a whisper from across a room. You need to be close to hear someone whisper to you. Don't waste valuable time fixing things because you didn't listen to your inner spirit resulting in hassles occupying your time! The *good spirit* is believing in God and his power to change and help us through our daily lives, and the *bad spirit* is believing in nothing and feeling alone and overwhelmed with no assurance of hope, simply enduring life. We bring others down that are exposed to our hopeless attitude. This is wrong and unfair to both yourself and those around you. Enjoy retirement and pay attention to the queues of others around you. This should be in conjunction with the awareness that God is watching how we handle our lives, our attitudes, and our gratefulness on a daily basis. It is not just fate that your circumstances are as they are. We create the world we live in and are ultimately responsible for the outcome of our lives. Using our intuition to guide our decisions in life and listening to our inner spirit, surrounding ourselves with the right people and controlling our thoughts will ultimately create your happiness in your life. What you practice you become good at.

Ask God to be in your heart and fill you with His spirit so your life can be enjoyed with less worry. Be bold and remind God of His promise as stated in the Bible, "I will never leave thee, nor forsake thee" (Hebrews 13:5, KJV).

Take time for yourself and realize you only have one body. You either own it healthy or you own it wrecked... either way you still own it! We will be happy if we are healthy! We will be healthy if we take the steps to make good decisions to do so.

We all have difficulties and struggles and challenges, but we make the mistake of allowing those circumstances to dictate our happiness. We can easily risk missing out on an abundant life. It was never God's intention for us to live one day on cloud nine and the next in the dumps because of our problems! Don't allow the future unknowns to make you anxious. When tomorrow comes, we will act how we *know* we should and take it day by day. Keep the goal of happiness and being who we are without allowing any outside influence. Run your own race!

I must give credit to *AARP* magazine for their different articles to draw from as a resource. (Nothing reminds me quicker about how old I am than by getting in the mail an *AARP* magazine!) Phil McGraw has written many good informative books about relationships and dysfunctions that were helpful. I would highly recommend any book he has written.

I also need to acknowledge many authors. A few of them are Richard Carlson, PhD; Spencer Johnson, MD; Susan Biali, MD; Tim Hansel; J. J. Virgin. I also enjoy Joel Osteen and Joyce Meyer with all of their perspective and understanding on issues and situations.

I have a plaque on my wall that says this: LIVE A GOOD LIFE, AND IN THE END, IT'S NOT THE YEARS IN THE LIFE. IT'S THE LIFE IN THE YEARS!

Future books to be written

"Fight the Fat After Fifty" and
"Saying Goodbye to a Long-Term Marriage"

Bibliography

Eric Klinenberg, PhD, author of *Going Solo*

Dr. Susan Forward, author of *Men Who Hate Women & the Women Who Love Them*

Dr. Phil McGraw, *Life Code*

Spencer Johnson, MD, *Yes or No: The Guide to Better Decisions*

Richard Carlson, PhD, *Don't Sweat the Small Stuff*

Paul Williams, PhD, of Lawrence Berkeley National Laboratory

Katherine Shear, MD, director of the Center for Complicated Grief at Columbia University School of Social Work in New York City

Thomas Goetz, a professor of empirical educational research at the University of Konstanz in Germany

Katherine Shear, MD, director of the Center for Complicated Grief at Columbia University School of Social Work in New York City.

Sarah A. Burgard, PhD, professor of sociology and epidemiology at the University of Michigan

Ross Miner, competitive figure skater

healthtools.aarp.org/health/kegel-exercises

Paul D. Nussbaum, PhD

J. J. Virgin, author of *Virgin Diet*

Pam Peeke, MD, MPH

Linda Young, PhD, a Washington-based therapist who specializes in helping women foster healthy relationships

Majid Fotuhi, MD, PhD, neurologist

Gary Small, MD, psychiatrist

Sue James, Maryland nutritionist

James Hagberg, PhD, professor of kinesiology at the University of Maryland

Bobbi Emel, a psychotherapist in Los Altos, California

Lee Schnebly, author of *I Do?*

2011 study in Strength and Conditioning Journal

Research from the US National Health Interview Study

AARP the magazine

The National Weight Control Registry

The Associated Press-Chicago

Contemporary Family Therapy Magazine, Researchers Michelle Jeanfreau, Anthony Jurich, Michael Mong